AdamLiawTwoAsianKitchens

AdamLiawTwoAsianKitchens

EBURY
PRESS

Contents

For my family. All over the world.

Introduction

Beginnings

Throughout my life I have been surrounded by different cultures. My father is Hainanese Chinese from Malaysia; my mother is Singaporean-born with English, French and Indonesian heritage. I was born in Penang, an island off north-west Malaysia that has a rich colonial history, and spent my youth in South Australia before living and working in Japan, China and India. Before I was 18 I had lived in more than 20 different homes across four countries, and each of their kitchens has left me with unique memories.

My eclectic upbringing has led me through some amazing food experiences. As a child, every week I would eat my way around the world: Hainanese chicken rice from my father's side; my grandmother's unforgettable Chinese and Malaysian classics; dishes from my mother's Singaporean childhood; and even traditional English roasts and puddings from my stepfather.

These foods sat together on our dining table, without care for combination or conflict, each representing a long and faithful culinary culture. English Yorkshire puddings with gravy and meat pies at the football are as much a childhood memory of mine as the sticky, black Hokkien noodles of Kuala Lumpur or the sour fishiness of Penang laksa. Most ethnic families would subscribe to a particular food culture as their own, but even though these dishes covered an impossibly wide spread of both geography and history, there was never a concept of food that was 'ours' and food we had 'borrowed' from another culture. The food we ate was simply the food we loved.

As I grew older I was able to explore Asia and experienced the cuisines of Vietnam, Japan, Korea, Thailand — and with each mouthful the dishes I ate became part of my own story. My fond memories of childhood food now sit happily next to those of oppressively spicy Korean bul dak washed down with a few beers and chamisuls with friends after work, late night okonomiyaki bought near my apartment in Tokyo, or the best grilled chicken from a Thai street market.

Culture, identity and food

The food we make is an expression of who we are and how we live our lives. My own family has crossed three countries in as many generations, and yet my story is not unique in Australia. We are truly lucky to have such an active and diverse migrant culture here. Migration has brought pasta, roast dinners and meat pies to Australia along with Cantonese barbecued pork, Thai curries and sushi. Teamed with amazing local produce, this has resulted in a vibrant and authentic range of global cuisines that is readily available just outside our front doors.

While the food we eat at home is an expression of who we are, the food we eat as a nation and the dishes that we make in our homes define 'Australian cuisine'. The same migratory forces that shaped Malaysian cuisine in the fourteenth century (through trade with Chinese merchants and British or Dutch colonials), Japanese cuisine in the sixteenth century (when the Portuguese introduced the local population to the forerunners of tempura and nanbanzuke), and Singaporean cuisine in the early twentieth century, are at work in Australia today, contributing to the development of an exciting national cuisine.

In the same way that the food of Mediterranean migrants has become part of our culture — and you'd be hard-pressed to find a single Australian family that doesn't include pasta or risotto as part of its kitchen repertoire — Asian food is already fundamental to what we eat in our restaurants. However, it's only just now becoming part of what we cook in our homes. Asian food is neither esoteric nor difficult, and Australians' love for Asian food is undeniable. Asian flavours and techniques will play a vital role in the future of our national cuisine.

The increase in Asian flavours in the food we eat should not be considered a threat to any existing food culture. Quite the contrary: it is the constant evolution of cultures, produce and flavours that underpins the strength of Australia's culinary future. From the talented world-class Australian chefs who inspire us, to the enthusiastic home cooks who feed our families every day, we all play our part in shaping that future.

温故知新

There is a Confucian proverb, which reads in part 'wen gu zhi xin' or, in Japanese, 'onko-chishin'. This translates roughly to 'consider old things to understand new things'. This is the essence of the Two Asian Kitchens.

We all strive for authenticity in our food; and true authenticity can only be achieved through an acute understanding of the history and meaning behind the food we cook. However, inherent within the goal of authenticity is the need for progress. Times, cultures, people and nations all change, and the food we eat must change with them. To rely on what has gone before is to deny the authenticity of the connection between food, produce and our daily lives. If we all ate exactly how our ancestors ate, the food in our daily lives would become an imitation of a different time. We need to grow and develop to maintain authenticity in the food we eat, but that does not mean rejecting our traditions. A faithful understanding of the history of food allows us to stand on the shoulders of giants and pioneer our own horizons.

The Two Asian Kitchens in my life are The Old Kitchen and The New Kitchen. They are concepts that explain the food I make and who I am. The Old Kitchen represents the traditional recipes from the many different cultures in which I have grown up, and with which I share a long personal history, while The New Kitchen represents a necessary spirit of creativity and expression; a desire to take the flavours, techniques and experiences of my past and help them grow and progress into the future.

The Old Kitchen

Within The Old Kitchen, you'll find hawker noodle dishes, Japanese yakitori, creamy coconut laksa and, my persistent favourite, Hainanese chicken rice. These are dishes that hold strong memories for me in time, place and emotion. They are the dishes of my history — the places I have been, the people I have met and the experiences I have had, and for me each of those meals is not simply a plate on a table. Hainanese chicken rice is not just a good lunch: it is the latest in a thousand delicious plates of chicken that my grandmother has lovingly prepared for our family. When I cook siew yuk, I am replaying the memory of my father carrying roasted pork belly home from the market on any of a hundred Saturday afternoons in Adelaide. A plate of beef with oyster sauce reminds me of all the times my mother served it up next to an equally huge platter of beef stroganoff to feed eight hungry children around the dinner table.

But these dishes, while intensely personal to me, all have long histories that reach back well before my time. That same plate of chicken rice made by my grandmother also tells the story of my grandfather's migration to Malaysia from Hainan Island off the southern coast of China. He was part of a wave of Hainanese migrants who sparked a period of intense innovation in Malaysian and Singaporean cuisine. Skilled chefs, these Hainanese migrants worked in Malay kitchens, often in the employ of the British colonials. The cuisine they developed knitted together the available local produce, the tastes of their British employers, their own culinary backgrounds, and the culture of the region. Initially a simple adaptation of the traditional Hainanese Wenchang chicken, only a few decades on from this period of creativity, that dish and others like it are now regarded as iconic dishes of Malaysian and Singaporean cuisine. They tell the story of their adopted home as eloquently as they tell the story of the place they first came from.

The New Kitchen

The New Kitchen features modern dishes that draw on the memorable flavours and experiences of my own life. While the Asian influences in my food are clear, I encourage you not to think of the dishes in The New Kitchen chapter as Chinese, Japanese or even as Asian in general. If you must classify the food of The New Kitchen, then think of it as Australian food. This is a book I have written as an Australian, in Australia, for Australians. The memories and experiences I have drawn on are my experiences as an Asian migrant in Australia.

I have loved food for as long as I can remember, but until I was 24 years old my cooking repertoire was limited to the faithful recreation of the dishes I had grown up with. As a child I had always watched my family in the kitchen and helped my mother with the evening meal. We ate at restaurants and I would hound my mother and grandmother to teach me how to cook my favourite dishes. One of my earliest food memories is of making a favourite dessert with my mother. The Chinese restaurant staple 'fried ice cream' was a regular treat for me and my brothers and sisters but, while I had enjoyed it for years at restaurants, I had never encountered anyone who had made it at home. The sense of achievement and pride at producing a reasonably credible version with my own two hands was a defining moment for me as an 8 year old. From that time I began to learn how to reproduce the dishes I loved to eat, and still the idea of creating new recipes seemed entirely unnecessary when there were so many traditional dishes I did not yet know.

When I moved to Japan at the age of 24 I was thrust into a wild new world. The produce was different, the kitchens were different and my experiences were different. I could no longer make do with cycling through my reliable repertoire of dishes from my past. At first I learnt the traditional Japanese recipes, tasting a new dish at a restaurant or a friend's home and then faithfully reproducing it in my own kitchen. But soon this was no longer enough — I understood these dishes and could make them well, but in doing so I felt almost robotic and uninspired. It was food that was connected to the place, but it was not yet connected to me.

It was at a second-hand sale in Shinagawa, Tokyo, that things changed. I bought a first edition of an old 1950s Californian cookbook entitled *Cooking Bold and Fearless* (a bargain at only 300 yen). This collection of recipes came from the *Sunset* magazines of the preceding decade and had been submitted by 'chefs-of-the-west' — food enthusiasts from all walks of life, from pilots and retired military officers, to plumbers and accountants. Post-war 1950s California was not somewhere I expected to find inspiration, but the recipes in this book showed pioneering spirit in exploring other cultures and foods. There were recipes for Spanish rice, Chinese ribs, Lebanese dips, Slavic borscht, Japanese tempura and French stews. While none of them were entirely traditional recipes, they all held a different kind of authenticity. This was food that meant something to its cooks; food that connected people to their time and their culture; and it was not a culture defined by geographic lines or the weight of simple history — it was the marriage of personal culture and food.

That book inspired me, not by its individual recipes alone but more by its spirit, to create new dishes that brought together my past and my present, and in doing so I discovered true authenticity in my own food. This was an authenticity that told my story. Of course, there were disasters — more than I would care to count — but good or bad, the food I started to make resonated with authenticity in a way that left me satisfied both in stomach and mind.

This book is not intended to be a definitive volume on the cuisines of Asia. The recipes of The Old Kitchen are dishes with which I have a strong relationship; they are dishes many of you will already know and have eaten. It is my hope that this book can be a seed of knowledge to demystify some of those recipes and help you bring them into your own kitchen.

Once armed with an understanding of the history and adventure behind the food of The Old Kitchen, the recipes of The New Kitchen are intended to inspire you to interpret, evolve and combine your own personal culture with the food you love to cook and eat.

Adam Liaw, 2011

In a restaurant, preparation is the most important factor in ensuring a smooth-running kitchen. The same principles can be applied to the home kitchen to take the stress out of preparing a meal for a hungry family.

While working full-time as a lawyer, I would still usually have time to cook breakfast, lunch and dinner. People would marvel at how this was possible. The secret (and it is not much of a secret) is to spend a few leisurely and relaxing hours each weekend making stocks, sauces and various pantry ingredients for the coming week. With sliced vegetables in the fridge and my everyday soup stock waiting in the freezer, making a healthy broth for breakfast would take 5 minutes. With meat already chopped, portioned and marinated, an evening stir-fry is only moments away.

While the final dish may take only a few minutes to make, the idea of a pantry full of basic ingredients you have made yourself goes a long way towards making your kitchen the living heart of your home.

Pantry

This is a stock that I make about once a week and use for almost everything. It's a great base for soups and soupy noodle dishes, or in stir-fries or simmered dishes. The more meat there is on the bones you use here, the more flavour there will be in the stock. I use a mixture of pork rib bones and chicken wings.

Everyday soup stock

Makes: 3 litres
Preparation: 10 minutes
Cooking: 1½–2 hours

750g chicken bones (or 750g chicken wings and
    bones, or 1 whole chicken)
750g pork bones (or pork ribs)
1 sheet (10cm square) kombu (dried kelp)
5 garlic cloves, unpeeled
2 thick slices ginger, bruised
6 spring onions, cut into 5cm lengths
½ brown onion, unpeeled
40g katsuoboshi (dried bonito flakes)

1. Place the bones (but not any meat cuts such as wings, ribs or whole chicken) in a deep stockpot and cover with cold water. Bring to the boil, skimming off any scum, and then pour off the water.

2. Using a dry cloth, wipe any visible dirt from the kombu but be careful not to wet it or wipe off any of the white powder on the surface.

3. Add any wings, ribs or other meat cuts to the bones in the stockpot and add the kombu, garlic, ginger, spring onions and brown onion. Cover with more cold water (3.5–4 litres) and place over medium heat. Once small bubbles start to break on the surface of the water, 1 bubble every 2 seconds, remove the kombu and lower the heat to maintain this temperature. Partially cover the pot and simmer for 1½ hours, making sure the stock never comes to the boil. If the stock boils, it will become cloudy. Skim regularly to remove any scum.

4. Turn off the heat and add the katsuoboshi. Place the stockpot into a sink full of iced water and leave to cool as quickly as possible (quick cooling prevents the stock spoiling when stored). Strain through a chinois lined with muslin and transfer to the fridge. When cold, remove any fat that has solidified on the surface. The cold stock will be cloudy but will clear when reheated.

Note: *You will note that this stock is not seasoned at any stage. Because it is so versatile I prefer to season it as I use it.*

Dashi is a base for simmered dishes, soups and sauces in Japanese cooking. The strong umami flavours in ichiban dashi ('first dashi') make it an ideal base for any number of savoury dishes.

This pickled daikon aims to create a crisp, clean flavour great for cooling spicy dishes or cutting through rich foods. The addition of gin and juniper berries accentuates the sharpness and clarity of flavour in the pickle.

Ichiban dashi

Makes: about 1.5 litres
Preparation: 5 minutes
Cooking: 5 minutes + 30 minutes standing

1 sheet (10cm square) kombu (dried kelp)
40g katsuoboshi (dried bonito flakes)

1. Using a dry cloth, wipe any visible dirt from the kombu but be careful not to wet it or wipe off any of the white powder on the surface.

2. Put the kombu and 1.5 litres water in a saucepan over medium heat. When the water starts to bubble at the bottom of the pan turn off the heat, remove the kombu and add the katsuoboshi. Leave for about 30 minutes until the katsuoboshi sinks to the bottom.

3. Strain the dashi through a fine muslin without squeezing the flakes. The dashi is best used as soon as possible but it will keep in the fridge for a week or so.

Notes: *If you like, you can reuse the katsuoboshi by adding it to 500ml water with an additional 15g of fresh katsuoboshi and bringing it to the boil. Simmer for a minute or two and then strain again. This produces niban dashi ('second dashi') which is less strongly flavoured than ichiban dashi.*

The white powder on the kombu is the source of its umami flavour, which is what makes a good dashi. Good-quality kombu has lots of powder on the surface. When making a stock as simple as dashi it's important to choose best-quality kombu and katsuoboshi.

White pickled daikon

Makes: 1 litre
Preparation: 15 minutes + 1 hour draining
Cooking: 5 minutes + overnight refrigeration

750g daikon, peeled and cut into 2cm cubes
100g sea salt flakes
250ml white vinegar
50ml gin
80g caster sugar
5 dried juniper berries, lightly crushed with a mortar and pestle

1. Toss the daikon and salt in a large bowl, then transfer to a colander to drain for 1 hour.

2. Sterilise two 500ml glass pickling jars and lids by running through a hot dishwasher or washing thoroughly and drying in a 110°C oven for 30 minutes. Rinse the daikon well, drain and pack tightly into the jars.

3. Put the remaining ingredients in a saucepan with 100ml water and bring to the boil. Remove from the heat and leave for a minute to cool slightly then slowly pour over the daikon (add gradually, to heat the jar slowly and prevent it cracking). Leave to cool and then put on the lids. Leave for at least 8 hours in the fridge before using.

from left: white pickled daikon; aromatic master stock; ichiban dashi; everyday soup stock

A master stock is an evolving, aromatic liquid used many times for poaching. As it is used, the flavour of the stock develops with the proteins cooked in it and, with good care, it will keep almost indefinitely in the freezer to be ready whenever called upon. Additional aromatics should be added periodically to keep the flavours strong, and the master stock must be taken out for a spin once in a while and brought to the boil to kill any bacteria that may want to grow. When poaching meat in my master stock, I often blanch in boiling water first to keep impurities out of the stock.

Aromatic master stock

Makes: about 1 litre
Preparation: 10 minutes
Cooking: 1 hour 10 minutes

750ml everyday soup stock (page 14)
2 tbsp neutral-flavoured oil
200g yellow rock sugar, crushed
200ml dark soy sauce
250ml Shaoxing wine
5 thick slices ginger, bruised
6 garlic cloves, unpeeled
6 spring onions, cut into 5cm lengths
½ brown onion, unpeeled, roughly chopped
2 cinnamon quills
4 whole star anise
1 tbsp Sichuan peppercorns
1 tbsp white peppercorns
1 tbsp fennel seeds
1 tbsp cloves
4 whole dried red chillies or 1 tbs dried chilli flakes
15g sea salt flakes

1. Bring the soup stock to a simmer in a large stockpot. Place a large wok over low heat, add the oil and rock sugar and stir until the sugar melts and then forms a dark, foamy caramel. Add a ladle or two of the soup stock and stir until the caramel dissolves — be careful, as the caramel will bubble up. Tip the contents of the wok into the simmering stock.

2. Add all the remaining ingredients and simmer, covered, for about 1 hour. Strain the master stock to remove all solids. Keep in an airtight container in the fridge, if using regularly, or in the freezer.

Cooking with master stock: *When poaching meat, poultry or seafood in master stock, it's best to keep pieces whole rather than slicing them before cooking. Blanch meat and poultry quickly in boiling water first to remove impurities, then simmer in the master stock over low heat until cooked. Lift out the meat, then bring the stock to the boil for a minute or two to kill any bacteria. I try to use my master stock weekly (thawing, cooking, re-boiling and re-freezing) and replenish liquids, aromatics and seasonings at least once a month.*

This is an easy bitter-sour lemon paste that I use to balance oily or sweet dishes. Meyer lemons are perfect because of their thin pith, but any lemons can be used. You can use a pressure cooker to speed up the process.

This simple, hot oil is brilliant with dumplings, poached meats, rice and noodle dishes, or just about anything really.

Lemon paste

Makes: about 150g
Preparation: 10 minutes
Cooking: 1 hour

4 lemons, preferably organic Meyer lemons

1. Scrub the lemon skins well to remove any wax and dirt. Put in a large saucepan and cover with plenty of cold water. Bring to the boil, cover and simmer for 1 hour.

2. Drain the lemons and cut in half. Remove any seeds but keep as much of the syrupy flesh as possible. Transfer to a food processor with the pith and skin.

3. Process to a smooth purée and then pass through a fine sieve. Store in an airtight container in either the fridge or freezer.

Chilli and garlic oil

Makes: 300ml
Preparation: 10 minutes
Cooking: 35 minutes

250ml neutral-flavoured oil
1 brown onion, finely chopped
5 garlic cloves, finely chopped
50g dried red chilli flakes
5g sea salt flakes

1. Heat 3 tablespoons of the oil in a wok or saucepan over low heat and fry the onion and garlic for about 3 minutes until translucent but not browned. Add the chilli flakes and fry for 1 minute. Add the salt and remaining oil.

2. Reduce the heat to very low and gently heat the chilli oil for about 30 minutes, stirring occasionally. Turn off the heat and leave to cool and infuse. When cooled, store in a jar.

from left: chilli and garlic oil; lemon paste; yuzu mayonnaise; curry laksa paste; sambal assam

Using a whole egg in this mayonnaise gives it a light texture that works well with seafood and fried foods. The yuzu juice provides great flavour and acidity.

This classic curry laksa paste is natural and preservative free, and can be stored for months in the freezer without spoiling. It's very simple but far superior in flavour and quality to most commercially produced pastes so please give it a try. I prefer to use fresh turmeric as powdered turmeric sometimes has a bitter flavour and often contains artificial colouring that gives an overly yellow colour to the laksa.

Yuzu mayonnaise

Makes: about 500ml
Preparation: 10 minutes

1 egg
2 tbsp yuzu juice
¼ tsp sea salt flakes
1 tsp caster sugar
500ml neutral-flavoured oil

1. Combine the egg, yuzu juice, salt and sugar in a small food processor. With the motor running, add the oil a few drops at a time at first, and then in a thin stream so that the oil emulsifies and does not separate from the egg mixture. The final mayonnaise should be thick and creamy, but still with a light texture.

Curry laksa paste

Makes: about 500ml
Preparation: 10 minutes + 20 minutes soaking

10 dried red chillies
2 tbsp dried shrimp
4 fresh long red chillies, deseeded
1 tbsp belacan (dried shrimp paste)
2 brown onions, roughly chopped
5 candlenuts (or macadamia nuts)
2 garlic cloves
2 thick slices ginger, peeled and chopped
2 stalks lemongrass (white part only), roughly chopped
5 Vietnamese mint leaves
1 tsp ground coriander
3 tsp grated fresh turmeric (or 1 tsp turmeric powder if absolutely necessary)
60ml peanut oil

1. Deseed the dried chillies by breaking off the stalk ends and shaking out the seeds or brushing them out with a wooden skewer. Combine the dried chillies and dried shrimp in a heatproof bowl and cover with boiling water. Soak for 20 minutes and then drain.

2. Mix the soaked chillies and shrimp with all the other ingredients in a food processor or mortar and process or pound to a very smooth paste. Store in an airtight container in the fridge or freezer.

A sambal is a spicy sauce containing chilli. There are many different types of sambal in South-East Asian cooking, but the addition of tamarind gives this sauce a great sourness that works well with seafood, white meat and even eggs. It is a perfect foil to coconut rice and is integral to the balance of many wonderful traditional dishes, such as nasi lemak.

Any fresh chillies can be used for this recipe. If you keep to one type of chilli per jar, you can choose the heat and colour of the chillies that you will be using in a final dish. That said, a mixture of different coloured chillies does make a pretty jar of pickles so even if I'm mixing colours I still try to keep to pickles of around the same heat.

Sambal assam

Makes: 300–350ml
Preparation: 10 minutes + 10 minutes standing
Cooking: 25 minutes

2 tbsp tamarind pulp
10 eschalots, roughly chopped
10 red chillies (any variety you like: I use a mixture of birds-eye for heat and large red chillies for colour)
4 garlic cloves, roughly chopped
100ml neutral-flavoured oil
60g palm sugar, roughly chopped
5g sea salt flakes
1 tsp belacan (dried shrimp paste), optional

1. Put the tamarind pulp in a heatproof bowl and add 250ml boiling water. Leave to cool, stirring occasionally, for about 10 minutes until the water is cool enough to touch comfortably. Strain the tamarind liquid, pressing the solids with the back of a spoon to extract as much liquid as possible. Scrape the bottom of the strainer into the liquid and discard the solids.

2. Combine the eschalots, chillies and garlic in a food processor and process to a rough paste. Heat the oil in a saucepan over medium heat, add the paste and reduce the heat to low. Cook the paste for 10–15 minutes, stirring regularly, until much of the moisture has evaporated and the mixture is fragrant.

3. Add the tamarind liquid, sugar, salt and belacan, if using. Cook, stirring occasionally, for 10–15 minutes until the red oil separates from the mixture. Store in an airtight container in the freezer.

Pickled chillies

Makes: 750ml
Preparation: 10 minutes
Cooking: 2 minutes

250g fresh chillies (any variety you like)
250ml rice wine vinegar
2 tbsp caster sugar
1 tbsp sea salt flakes

1. Sterilise a 750ml glass pickling jar and lid by running it through the dishwasher or washing thoroughly and then drying in a 110°C oven for 30 minutes.

2. Wash and slice the chillies, then place in a bowl, cover with boiling water and leave for 5 minutes. Use a slotted spoon to transfer the chillies to the jar, packing them to the top and leaving as many seeds behind as you can.

3. Bring the vinegar, caster sugar and salt to the boil in a small saucepan. Leave for a minute or so to cool and then slowly pour over the chillies (add gradually, to heat the jar slowly). Tap the jar to bring any air bubbles to the top, allow to cool and then put on the lid. Refrigerate for at least 8 hours before using.

clockwise from top right: pickled chillies; teriyaki glaze; mentsuyu; yakitori tare; tentsuyu

Tentsuyu is a Japanese dipping sauce for tempura and other fried foods. Its light, clean flavour and texture can be enhanced by adding a little grated daikon just before serving.

Mentsuyu is a Japanese dipping sauce for cold noodles, but it can also be used as a flavour base for stir-fries and other dishes. When eaten with cold noodles, mentsuyu is flavoured with piquant or savoury elements such as spring onions, ginger or dried seaweed just before serving.

Tentsuyu

Makes: about 350ml
Preparation: 5 minutes
Cooking: about 5 minutes

60ml mirin
2 tsp caster sugar
250ml ichiban dashi (page 15)
60ml light soy sauce

1. Combine the mirin and sugar in a saucepan and stir over medium heat until the sugar has dissolved. Add the dashi and soy sauce and bring to a simmer. Leave to cool to room temperature before using.

Mentsuyu

Makes: about 650ml
Preparation: 5 minutes
Cooking: about 5 minutes

500ml ichiban dashi (page 15)
80ml mirin
80ml light soy sauce

1. Combine all ingredients in a small saucepan and bring to a simmer. Leave to cool to room temperature before serving.

Every yakitori restaurant in Japan will have their own yakitori tare (pronounced tah-ray) that is unique to the master of the store. This is my version but yours should be personal to you, so don't be afraid to substitute ingredients or add others, depending on your tastes.

In Japanese 'teriyaki' means 'glazed grill' and, as such, should be considered a glaze rather than a sauce. This is an excellent match for many different kinds of meat, poultry and seafood. I like to add molasses to my teriyaki for a certain complexity of flavour and to prevent the crystallisation of sugars. If you don't have any sake, you can use a light, dry white wine instead.

Yakitori tare

Makes: about 900ml
Preparation: 15 minutes
Cooking: 1 hour

1 chicken carcass (about 500g)
400ml dark soy sauce
150ml light soy sauce
350ml sake
200ml mirin
200g yellow rock sugar
2 strips lemon zest
1 tbsp molasses, optional

1. Preheat the oven to 220°C and roast the chicken carcass for 30 minutes until golden brown. Transfer to a large saucepan and add the remaining ingredients. Bring to a simmer over medium heat, stirring to dissolve the sugar.

2. Reduce the heat to low and simmer for about 30 minutes, until the mixture has reduced by one quarter. Allow to cool and then remove the zest and chicken carcass. Strain the liquid and store in an airtight container in the fridge.

Teriyaki glaze

Makes: about 700ml
Preparation: 5 minutes
Cooking: 2 minutes

250ml dark soy sauce
200ml mirin
200ml sake
60g caster sugar
2 tbsp molasses

1. Place all ingredients in a saucepan and stir over low heat, without ever bringing to the boil, until the sugar has dissolved. Cool and store in the fridge.

Too often we tell ourselves that there is much in the kitchen we cannot do, or that our skills do not extend to certain areas. Within this chapter the techniques of Asian cooking are shown as they are: simple and elegant. They do not require any special training or skill to execute well. There is little more to a stir-fry than combining ingredients over high heat to let their natural flavours come forward, and there is no more mystery to a dumpling than a delicious filling wrapped in pastry.

I encourage you to look at ways you can use these techniques to interpret your own tastes, and to think about using the ingredients you love in new ways. Every new technique learned can open the door to a hundred new dishes.

OnTechniques

On donburi

Rice bowl (donburi translates as 'bowl') dishes are some of my favourite meals in Japan. While most traditional Japanese meals consist of a number of small shared dishes, the donburi is an entire meal served in a bowl. Donburi first originated as a labourers' meal so that workers could eat quickly without the rigmarole of a more formal meal service. For me, there is nothing I like more than sitting down on the couch with a donburi. In my kitchen I always keep my favourite rice bowl on hand for when the urge strikes.

Although donburi have been popularised by cheap cafeterias and chain restaurants, there is a real art to finding the perfect mix of flavours and textures to create an entire meal in a bowl. A good donburi can be as simple as grilled marinated meat with some pickles or condiments, or a simple stir-fry of egg and tomatoes served over rice. Enjoy the donburi recipes in this book, or experiment and create your own rice bowls.

Tips for donburi

- The most important part of a donburi is the rice itself. The rice must be cooked perfectly with grains separate for good texture but still sticky enough to hold together and be eaten with chopsticks. Use short-grain rice for best results.

- The topping should contain enough moisture to drip down and flavour the rice.

- The weight of the rice and topping should be balanced with a touch of lightness in the form of a condiment, some fresh greenery or even toasted nori.

- Find a beautiful bowl and keep it in your kitchen cupboard, only for donburi.

Perfectly cooked rice

(Makes about 3 cups of perfectly cooked rice)

2 cups short-grain rice (other types of rice
   can be used)

3 cups water

1. Put the rice in a colander or sieve and wash
   under running water until the water runs
   clear. Set aside for 30 minutes. Put the rice
   and water in a small heavy-based saucepan
   with a tight-fitting lid. Bring to a simmer,
   uncovered, then continue to simmer for
   about 5 minutes until the water is level with
   the top of the rice and tunnels appear in the
   rice where steam is escaping.

2. Put the lid on the pan, reduce the heat to
   very low and leave for 10 minutes. Remove
   from the heat and leave to stand for a
   further 5 minutes. Remove the lid and use a
   moistened rice paddle or wooden spoon to
   fluff the rice and drive off any excess steam.

Some popular donburi

- *Oyako-don* ('parent and child bowl')
  This playful name refers to the relationship
  between the two main ingredients of
  chicken and egg. Chicken is simmered in a
  mixture of soy, dashi, mirin and sugar. Eggs
  are added and cooked until semi-set and
  then served over rice.

- *Tanin-don* ('stranger bowl')
  Beef is substituted for chicken in this recipe
  and the name reflects the disconnect
  between the cow and the egg.

- *Gyu-don* ('beef bowl')
  Beef strips are fried and simmered in a
  sweet sauce with onions, served over rice
  and eaten with red pickled ginger.

- *Katsu-don* ('pork cutlet bowl')
  This popular pork cutlet recipe (page 77) is
  also one of my favourites.

- *Ten-don* ('tempura bowl')
  Tempura prawns are placed on top of the
  rice and a few tablespoons of tentsuyu
  (Pantry, page 26) is added flavour and
  moisten the dish.

- *Maguro-don* ('tuna bowl')
  Raw tuna is placed on top of the rice and
  moistened with soy sauce (or a mixture of
  soy sauce and sake). The dish is freshened
  with a little wasabi.

On dumplings

There is an entire galaxy of different dumplings — wontons, potstickers, xiaolongbao, gyoza — but many of these varieties follow the same basic recipe for a simple pork mince filling.

The secret to a good dumpling is a firm, consistent and moist filling. Some homemade fillings can be grainy and dry. A delicious, springy dumpling needs a fine mince with enough fat to keep it moist. Pork mince is best, but most pre-minced pork is too coarse and doesn't contain enough fat. I mince my own meat from pork belly mixed with pork shoulder, for good fat content. If you use pre-minced pork, pass it through a mincer or process all or half in a food processor until finely ground.

My grandmother says to mix the dumpling filling in one direction only. This old wives' method actually fulfils a vital purpose through a chemical process called thermo-gelling. Muscle fibres in meat and fish contain myofibrillary proteins known as actin and myosin. When heated in solution, these proteins form a gel which traps water, fat and starch to create a springy, moist filling.

This basic pork filling can be used as it is, but I divide it into smaller portions and mix each with a different flavour — garlic chives, shiso (perilla), shiitake mushrooms, water chestnuts, fresh herbs, pea shoots, chilli paste, chopped prawns or even chopped gelatinous soup that has been chilled until set (this produces soup-filled dumplings).

You can use bought wrappers but a simple boiling water dumpling dough is so easy to make that it's hardly worth a trip to the supermarket. I fold each flavour into a different shape and keep a good supply in the freezer. I eat dumplings as a snack with chilli and garlic oil (Pantry, page 19) and Chinkiang black vinegar, or in a broth to make dumpling soup.

Basic pork dumpling filling

1kg fatty pork, finely minced
1 cup finely chopped and blanched
    Chinese cabbage
2 garlic cloves, finely chopped
2 tsp grated ginger
1 tbsp white vinegar
2 tbsp cornstarch
1 tsp salt
¼ tsp white pepper

1. Mix all the ingredients together and knead firmly for about 10 minutes to release the myofibrillary protein and produce the gel for a moist filling. Refrigerate for 30 minutes. Use as is, or add other flavourings now.

Boiling water dumpling dough

4 cups plain flour (or plain flour mixed with
    wheaten cornflour)
2 cups boiling water

1. Sift the flour into a large bowl and make a well in the centre. Pour in the boiling water and mix with a wooden spoon until it comes together. Knead the dough for about 5 minutes until silky, then cover with plastic wrap and rest for 30 minutes.

2. Roll out the dough into long snakes and then cut into lengths about half the size of a ping-pong ball. Roll each ball from the edge to the centre to make a circle, turning the dough 90 degrees after every roll. After about 8 turns you should have a perfectly round, very thin wrapper. Place 1 teaspoon filling in the middle and fold into shape.

Folding, storing and cooking

I won't attempt to explain the more complex folding methods in print, save to say that the shape of the dumpling will often give a good indication of the best way to cook it. I usually fry-steam dumplings (see below) so I fold them in a gyoza shape, but simpler folds are fine for dumplings that will be boiled.

For a very simple folded dumpling that looks fine boiled or in soup, place about 1 teaspoon of filling in the centre of the wrapper. Dip your finger in water and wet the edge of the top half of the wrapper and fold the bottom half up into a half-moon shape. Make sure that the filling is centred and that there is no air trapped in the wrapper. Pinch the edges to seal. You can leave them as half moons, like some Japanese or Korean dumplings, or wet the very top of the half-moon and fold each pointy end up to the centre.

Place the filled dumplings on a tray, making sure they don't touch each other. When a batch is finished, transfer the tray to the freezer. When frozen, transfer each batch to a large ziplock bag marked with the flavour. Store in the freezer.

Dumplings can be cooked from frozen by several different methods. Boil in salted water or stock for about 7 minutes. Or steam for 10–12 minutes. Deep-fry dumplings in hot oil. Or fry-steam them (as for gyoza) by browning in a little hot oil in a frying pan, then adding water to the pan to come halfway up the dumplings. Cook until the water has evaporated and the dumplings are left to fry again.

On sushi

It is often said in Japan that, when an apprentice trains to become a sushi chef, it takes three years to master nigiri sushi, five years to master maki zushi and 10 years to become a fully-fledged sushi chef. Great sushi is certainly an art, but you can make perfectly serviceable sushi at home with just a little bit of practice.

The most important component of good sushi is the rice itself. Good-quality Japanese short-grain rice is essential — as is achieving a good balance of sweetness, saltiness and vinegar in the seasonings.

Sushi is traditionally accompanied by wasabi, pickled ginger and tea. Fresh wasabi is far superior to the powdered stuff or pre-mixed tubes. If you can't find fresh wasabi a good alternative is wasabi powder mixed with finely grated daikon radish.

Sushi rice

4 cups Japanese short-grain rice
125ml rice wine vinegar
50g caster sugar
5g salt
1 large piece kombu (dried kelp)

1. Wash the rice well and leave for 1 hour. Mix the vinegar, sugar and salt in a small saucepan and stir over heat until the sugar has dissolved. Cool to room temperature.

2. Brush any dirt from the kombu with a dry cloth but do not wash or brush away any of the white powder (this is the natural glutamate that provides the umami flavour to the rice).

3. Put the rice and kombu in a heavy-based saucepan with a tight-fitting lid. Add 1 litre of cold water and bring to a simmer over medium heat, then remove the kombu.

4. Simmer until the water is level with the top of the rice and tunnels appear in the top of the rice where steam is escaping. Reduce the heat to very low and put the lid on the pan. Steam for 10 minutes and then remove from the heat. Leave for a further 5 minutes without uncovering.

5. Brush a bamboo basin, roasting tray or other large flat tray with sides with a little of the vinegar mixture. Tip the rice into the basin. Fan the rice to drive off excess moisture and cool it quickly, while turning it with a bamboo spatula in a cutting motion. Sprinkle the vinegar mixture over the rice a little at a time, fanning and cutting the rice until it reaches blood temperature. Cover with a piece of dampened muslin.

Popular sushi

- *Chirashi* ('scattered sushi')
  Chirashi zushi is the easiest of all sushi to make. As the name implies, ingredients are simply scattered over a bed of rice, a little soy or wasabi is added and it's ready to go.

- *Maki* ('rolled sushi')
  Rolled sushi is the most widely known of the sushi shapes, popularised by chains of sushi bars in the west. Western versions of these rolls often contain a long list of ingredients, while the traditional Japanese versions usually contain only one ingredient in thin rolls (hosomaki) or up to three ingredients in fat rolls (futomaki).

- *Temaki* ('hand-rolled sushi')
  For temaki sushi, a half sheet of nori is covered in rice and filling and rolled by hand into a cone shape.

- *Nigiri* ('grabbed sushi')
  Nigiri sushi is made by squeezing rice into a firm torpedo shape in the palm of the hand. The rice is then topped usually with a smear of wasabi and an ingredient such as a slice of fish or a slice of Japanese omelette. Nigiri sushi is usually eaten with soy sauce — the piece is dipped into the soy sauce upside down (ingredient first) so that the rice does not soak up too much of the sauce.

- *Temari* ('balled sushi')
  Temari sushi is a very simple form of sushi. The rice is rolled into a small ball and topped with the chosen ingredient, usually a small slice of raw fish. Temari sushi is similar to nigiri sushi but is generally considered easier to make.

- *Gunkan* ('battleship sushi')
  Gunkan sushi takes its name because its shape is reminiscent of ancient Japanese warships. A small oval of rice is surrounded by a high collar of nori and then filled with soft ingredients such as salmon roe, sea urchin, oysters or natto.

- *Inari*
  To make inari zushi, a pouch of sweet, simmered, fried tofu is filled with sushi rice and sometimes other ingredients. Inari zushi is named for the Shinto god Inari, whose helper takes the shape of a fox and is supposed to have a fondness for this kind of tofu.

On stir-frying

Stir-frying is the cornerstone of any Asian kitchen and will enhance the texture and flavour of food. Stir-frying often produces Maillard reactions: the browning reactions that occur during the cooking of amino acids in proteins and naturally reducing sugars to produce brown, flavourful compounds. (These compounds are responsible for many of our favourite tastes — from the brown crust on cakes to the heady aromas of a Sunday roast, espresso coffee or brewed beer.) Maillard reactions have been part of Chinese kitchen theory for centuries and are historically known as 'wok hei', a Cantonese expression meaning 'spirit of the wok'.

Choosing a wok

For me, perfect stir-frying conditions come from a round-bottomed, hand-beaten carbon steel wok over a gas wok ring. Let me explain:

Materials Carbon steel has the best balance of durability, weight, heat retention and conductivity. Aluminium and non-stick woks are best avoided; aluminium because it damages easily and can taint the food, and non-stick because it should not be used at the high heat required for true stir-frying.

Construction Multi-ply and hand-beaten construction give strength and rigidity, while hand beating provides texture on the inside slope so that food is easily distributed around the varying heat zones. Round-bottomed woks provide the best control over heat (and, while flat-bottomed woks are better for induction and electric stoves, they are best avoided).

Heat source Stir-frying needs direct high heat. You can remove the standard burner cover on a domestic gas stovetop and replace it with a wok holder. Electric or induction cooktops do not have the necessary spread of direct heat.

Seasoning and cleaning your wok

A well-used wok has a characteristic brown-black patina. Seasoning before use produces a natural, polymerised, non-stick surface. Before using a new wok, follow these steps:

1. Clean the wok with detergent and rinse well. Dry the wok and heat for 5–10 minutes over medium heat until the metal turns blue-black with tinges of yellow. This ensures that the wok is dry and expands the metal so that it will easily coat with the fat.

2. Brush the wok with a thin layer of linseed oil (a drying oil) or an oil high in saturated fats, such as lard, palm oil or coconut oil. Heat for 10 minutes over medium heat and then wipe with paper towel. Repeat the brushing and wiping 3–4 more times until there is no black residue left on the towel. Your wok is now seasoned and ready to use.

3. After each use, clean the wok with water only: you should not need to scrub or use detergent. Dry over heat and wipe with a very small amount of oil to coat before storing. Over time your wok should gain a strong, non-stick seasoned coating.

Basic stir-fry marinade

1 tbsp light soy sauce
1 tsp cornflour
1 tsp Shaoxing rice wine, sherry or mirin
1 pinch white pepper

Mix together all the ingredients in a non-reactive dish. Add about 250g of thinly sliced meat and leave to marinate.

Some tips for stir-frying

- Choose your meat well and slice it yourself. Choose a flavoursome cut from a well-raised animal and slice thinly across the grain. I like rump or topside for beef; belly, leg or neck for pork; or thigh for chicken. Seafood should be of the best quality.

- Heat the wok until very hot, then add the room temperature oil in a circular motion, letting it run down to the base. I find a squeeze bottle useful for this.

- Add any garlic or ginger to the oil first and fry until just starting to brown. Remove with your wok tool and set aside. Add the meat to the flavoured oil and toss until browned. Remove the meat and set aside. You can reintroduce the garlic, ginger and meat to the wok at the end of cooking.

- Add the vegetables in order of how long they take to cook — the slower cooking ones need to be added first so that everything is ready at the same time.

- Never overcrowd your wok: the ingredients will steam and braise rather than frying.

- A good stir-fry does not need lots of strong sauces or flavourings. Try adding just salt and a little stock to let the natural flavours of your ingredients come through.

- Don't be afraid to thicken any collected sauce with a little cornflour slurry (cornflour mixed with cold water). This will coat the ingredients and give a tastier dish. Cook the thickened sauce for at least 30 seconds, to clarify. And let your stir-fry sit for a minute before serving to allow the flavours to come together and any sauce to thicken slightly.

On fruit liquors

Preserving is something of a lost art in today's kitchen. In the past this was a vital skill that made the most of ingredients in season. As we think more about sustainability of our food sources and availability of seasonal ingredients, it makes sense to relearn this skill.

One of my favourite ways to use fruit in season is to flavour alcohol. Japanese 'umeshu' is made by steeping unripe ume (sometimes called Japanese plum or Japanese apricot) in a lightly flavoured white liquor until the fruit yields its flavour and colour to the liquid. All manner of fruit can be used. The fruit liquor can be drunk neat, over ice or mixed with a little soda or warm water.

While the tasty fruit liquor is the goal here, the alcohol-macerated fruit is also edible. Use it as you would a Bachelor's jam — as a topping for desserts or stirred through cream or ice cream.

Japanese shochu is a distilled alcohol made from barley, wheat, potato, buckwheat, rice or even brown sugar. The flavours vary widely but a more mildly flavoured alcohol is perfect for fruit liquor. Shochu is available in Australia, or you could substitute vodka, brandy or rum.

For stone fruits, choose fruit that is just not quite ripe enough to eat — the firm flesh holds better in the alcohol. The addition of lemon zest to many fruits will balance the sweetness of the fruit sugars with the alcohol, but ultimately the choice of fruit, the amount of sugar and whether or not you add lemon zest is just a matter of personal preference.

Preparing the fruit

- *Oranges, limes and lemons* Pare off the zest with a peeler or paring knife, then peel any pith away from the flesh. Use the flesh and zest and discard the pith. Use about 300g of ice sugar per 1kg. Strain off the zest and flesh after 1–2 weeks. As an alternative, you can use the zest only.

- *Lychees* Peel the lychees and use about 300g of ice sugar per 1kg (for a very sweet liquor).

- *Apricots* Choose under-ripe apricots and remove any remains of the stalks with a skewer. Wash well and allow to air dry. Use about 300g of ice sugar per 1kg.

- *Peaches* Choose under-ripe peaches. Wash well and prick the skins with a skewer. The flavour of peaches works well with vanilla. Use about 300g of ice sugar per 1kg.

- *Kiwifruit* Peel the fruit and cut in half. Add the zest of 3 lemons. Use 250g of ice sugar per 1kg. Remove the zest after 1–2 weeks.

- *Pineapple* Peel the pineapple and cut into chunks. Add the zest of 2 lemons. Use 200g of ice sugar per 1kg. Remove the zest after 1–2 weeks.

- *Strawberries* Wash well and remove the stalks with a knife. Add the zest of 4 lemons. Use 300g ice sugar per 1kg. Remove the zest after 1–2 weeks.

- *Cherries* Wash well and remove the stalks. Prick the skins a few times with a skewer. Cherries work very well with brandy; add a few sticks of cinnamon for a unique flavour. Use 150g of ice sugar per 1kg.

- *Apples* There is no need to peel the apples, but remove the cores and cut them into large chunks. I use Granny Smith apples for their tartness. Galas have a honey flavour, so add a little honey with the sugar. Add the zest of 2–3 lemons, and/or some fresh herbs such as shiso leaf (perilla) or mint. Use about 150g of ice sugar per 1 kg to keep the flavour fresh and tart.

Basic fruit liquor

1kg prepared fruit
4-litre airtight glass preserving container
ice sugar (as above)
2 litres of your preferred alcohol (shochu, vodka, rum or brandy)

1. Wash 1kg fruit well and prepare as above. Clean and dry your container.

2. Put half the ice sugar in the container and add half the fruit. Add the rest of the sugar, then the rest of the fruit. Add the alcohol until the fruit is completely covered. It doesn't matter if some of the fruit is floating — it will sink over time.

3. Seal the jar tightly and store in a cool, dark place for at least 2 months. Most liquors are drinkable after about 2 months but longer maturation will allow the flavours to mellow. After 6 months, the fruit can be strained off and the alcohol bottled and left to mature even longer, if you like.

On tempura

Tempura originated in Japan from the deep-frying techniques carried there by Portuguese merchant sailors and missionaries in the early 17th century. It is even suggested that the name tempura comes from Quattuor Tempora — the times in the religious calendar when Catholics were forbidden meat, and so ate seafood. Deep-fried dishes were common in Portuguese cuisine and this deep-fried seafood eaten at certain religious times became known as tempura. When Japanese monks applied the same battering process to vegetables, this became known as shojin-age (from the Japanese term for Buddhist vegetarian cuisine).

Today, the distinction between tempura and shojin-age has been lost and the term tempura refers to any seafood or vegetable coated in a light batter and deep-fried until crispy.

The secret to light, crisp tempura batter is not to activate or work the gluten in the flour. Using a low-gluten flour is best as Australian flour tends to be higher in gluten then its Japanese counterpart. Failing that, mix a few tablespoons of wheaten cornflour with your plain flour to reduce the gluten content.

Preparing seafood and vegetables

For tempura I like to use white-fleshed seafood such as prawns, squid, scallops, clams and thin white fish such as whiting and garfish. Score deep grooves in the underside of prawns to prevent them curling during frying.

Any vegetables can be used, but I particularly like carrot, eggplant, sweet potato, onion, pumpkin, lotus root, capsicum and fresh shiitake and enoki mushrooms. Slice the vegetables no thicker than 5mm, or make 'kakiage' by mixing together various julienned vegetables and/or seafood.

You can also try tempura batter on herbs such as shiso, basil and mint. Batter only one side of the leaf (so that the coating is not too thick) and deep-fry for just a few seconds.

Basic tempura batter

1 cup low-gluten flour or plain
   flour mixed with 2 tsbp wheaten cornflour
1 egg
1 cup chilled soda water
5 ice cubes
a little extra flour, to dust

1. Put the flour in a bowl, or mix together the flour and wheaten cornflour. In another bowl, mix the egg and soda water. Combine the two mixtures and gently draw a pair of chopsticks through until the batter is just combined but still lumpy. Add the ice cubes and keep chilled in the fridge. (The combination of soda water, lumps in the batter and cold temperature will produce carbon dioxide when added to hot oil. The release of this gas from the batter will give you a crisp and crunchy tempura.)

2. Heat vegetable or sunflower oil in a wok or deep wide pan (traditionally sesame oil was used, but that is not practical in many kitchens today). I fry seafood at 180°C and vegetables, which take a little longer to cook, at 165°C.

3. Dust the seafood or vegetables with a little flour. Draw them through the batter to lightly coat and then add to the hot oil (I use a pair of long cooking chopsticks). Hold the tempura in the oil for a few moments before releasing it, to start the frying process and prevent the tempura sinking to the bottom of the oil. Deep-fry until cooked through but only lightly coloured. Lift out and drain on a wire rack — the circulating air ensures that the batter remains crisp.

4. As bits of batter float to the surface during cooking, skim these off and keep them. These are known as 'tenkasu' and are used in dishes such as okonomiyaki, udon noodle soups and even some desserts (page 212).

5. Place the tempura on folded paper on a plate. In Japan, the paper is a sign of the quality of the tempura — well cooked tempura leaves no oil on the paper. Serve with tentsuyu (Pantry, page 26) or with good sea salt, either on its own or flavoured by pounding with powdered green tea, curry powder or other flavourings.

The Old Kitchen are the dishes that drive
the soul of my food. Many of these recipes
are from my past and from my family. They
are the classic dishes of Asia, rich with
the history of a region and its people. The
mixture of Indian and Chinese flavours in
Malacca's Ayam Kapitan are reminders of a
time of political intrigue, industry and power
that reach back 600 years. The flavours and
techniques of the Okinawan kitchen speak of
a thousand years of history with Japan and
China alongside 50 years of contemporary
post-war US occupation.

These national cuisines tell the story of the
country, but for all of us the food we choose
to cook and eat tells our own story. Whether
it's a family recipe passed from father to
daughter, or a dish that conjures memories
of a romantic holiday years past, our culinary
soul is born from our own personal history.

TheOldKitchen

This Japanese vegetarian dish is a flavoursome and healthy alternative to white or fried rice. Serve with a few small salads or cooked dishes or as a meal in itself. Konnyaku jelly is made from the konnyaku yam and is extremely low in fat and calories while relatively high in fibre and minerals. It is quite firm and doesn't dissolve when heated — its texture makes it a great addition to this dish so it's worth tracking down.

Kayaku gohan
(healthy vegetable rice)

Serves: 4–6 as a side dish
Preparation: 20 minutes
Cooking: about 25 minutes

6 dried shiitake mushrooms
50g konnyaku jelly
1 small carrot
440g Japanese short-grain rice
1 sheet (10cm square) kombu (dried kelp)
45g deep-fried tofu, cut into strips
3 tbsp light soy sauce
2 tbsp sake
1 tbsp mirin
¼ tsp grated ginger
1 tsp sea salt flakes
sliced nori or spring onion, to serve

1. Put the mushrooms in a heatproof bowl and cover with boiling water. Soak for 15 minutes to soften, then drain. Discard the stems and thinly slice the caps.

2. Meanwhile, put the konnyaku jelly in a small saucepan and cover with cold water. Bring to the boil and simmer for 2–3 minutes. Remove from the water, cool and cut into batons about 2cm long. Cut the carrot into similar sized batons.

3. Wash the rice and place in a large heavy-based saucepan. Cover with 750ml water and add the mushroom, konnyaku, carrot, kombu, tofu, soy sauce, sake, mirin, ginger and salt. Stir together well. Bring to a simmer over medium heat and remove the kombu. Simmer for 5 minutes and then cover with a tight-fitting lid and leave for 15 minutes over very low heat. Set aside for a further 5 minutes without removing the lid.

4. Tip out the rice into a large tray or bowl (a bamboo rice tub is ideal) and turn with a cutting motion (as you would sushi rice) to drive off the steam and cool the rice slightly. After a minute or two the rice should be ready to serve. Scatter with a little dried nori or sliced spring onion, or serve just as it is.

Note: *Burdock is traditionally added to this recipe with the carrot. It is often available, frozen, at Japanese grocers. If you can find it, use 50g thinly shaved burdock.*

*Less of a curry than a dry spiced coconut stew,
rendang is a classic Malaysian and Indonesian dish.
Serve it simply with plain rice or together as part of
a plate of nasi lemak.*

Beef rendang

Serves: 4–6
Preparation: 30 minutes
Cooking: about 2 hours

1 tbsp neutral-flavoured oil
1kg chuck steak, beef short rib or other
    braising steak, cut into 3cm cubes
3 stalks lemongrass, white part only,
    bruised with a pestle
1 turmeric leaf, shredded (or 3 kaffir lime
    leaves, shredded)
2 tsp sugar
400ml coconut cream
100g grated fresh coconut

Base paste
8 eschalots
6 red birds-eye chillies
6 garlic cloves
3cm piece each of galangal, ginger and
    turmeric, all peeled and thickly sliced
2 tsp sea salt flakes

1. To make the base paste, put all the ingredients in a food processor or mortar and grind to a fairly smooth paste.

2. Heat the oil in a large saucepan and fry the paste, stirring often, over medium heat for about 5 minutes until darkened and fragrant.

3. Add the beef, lemongrass, turmeric leaf and sugar and toss to coat in the paste. Add the coconut cream and 250ml water and bring to a low simmer. Cover and cook for 30 minutes, then uncover and cook for 1 hour. In this time the coconut cream should split to release its oil while the liquid boils away. The cooking process will turn from simmering to frying to give a flavoursome dry dish. If the liquid is evaporating too quickly, cover the pot for a while or add a little more water.

4. Meanwhile, dry-fry the coconut in a frying pan until golden brown. Transfer to a mortar and grind to a paste. The coconut will release its oil during grinding and the paste will become sticky.

5. When the beef has been cooking for 1½ hours and most of the liquid has evaporated, add the coconut paste and cook, stirring often, over low heat for 30 minutes until the liquid has evaporated and the meat is frying in the separated coconut oil. Adjust the seasoning and serve.

Note: *Substitute 130g desiccated coconut for the grated fresh coconut, if necessary.*

This is my favourite food to eat in the world. My grandfather emigrated to Malaysia from Hainan Island in the south of China in the 1920s. Like many Hainanese immigrants, my grandfather was a cook. The skill of these Hainanese cooks in fusing local cuisine with Chinese flavours and British colonial tastes became fundamental to Malaysian cooking. This dish is based on the traditional Wenchang chicken of Hainan Island, and I like to think (rather romantically) that my own family perhaps played a part in its history.

Hainanese chicken rice

Serves: 4
Preparation: 1 hour
Cooking: 50 minutes + 30 minutes standing

1 whole chicken (about 1.5 kg), at room temperature
5 whole garlic cloves, plus 2 cloves, chopped
7 thick slices ginger, unpeeled
1 tbsp sesame oil
675g jasmine rice
½ tsp sea salt flakes
1 tbsp light soy sauce
coriander, sliced cucumber and sliced spring onion, to serve

Chilli sauce
6 red birds-eye chillies
2 tbsp grated ginger
2 garlic cloves
1 tsp caster sugar
¼ tsp sea salt flakes
1 tsp lemon juice

Spring onion and ginger oil
4 spring onions, thinly sliced
2 tbsp grated ginger
½ tsp sea salt flakes
3 tbsp neutral-flavoured oil

Dressing
1 tbsp sesame oil
2 tbsp light soy sauce

1. Trim any visible fat from the chicken. Roughly chop the fat and put in a small saucepan. Cook over very low heat for about 1 hour until the liquid fat renders away. Pour off and keep the liquid fat as it pools. (You do not need the crispy pieces of fried fat for this dish, but they are excellent served over cooked noodles.)

2. Meanwhile, put the whole garlic cloves and 5 slices of ginger in the cavity of the chicken and place breast-side-down in a large pot. Cover with water and bring to a low simmer. Simmer for 25 minutes, then cover the pot and turn off the heat. Leave for 30 minutes, then lift out the chicken, keeping the poaching stock. Brush the chicken skin with sesame oil and wrap with plastic wrap.

3. Heat 1 tbsp of the chicken fat in a large saucepan over medium heat. Add the chopped garlic and remaining 2 slices of ginger and stir-fry until fragrant. Add the rice and toss until well coated and turning opaque. Add 1.25 litres of the reserved chicken stock, the salt and soy sauce. Follow the instructions to make perfectly cooked rice, page 31. Alternatively, fry the rice first in a wok and then transfer to a rice cooker.

4. To make the chilli sauce, combine chillies, ginger, garlic, sugar and salt in a mortar and pound to a paste. Add the lemon juice and 1–2 tablespoons of hot chicken stock and pound again. Set aside.

5. To make the spring onion and ginger oil, add the spring onion, ginger and salt to a heatproof mortar and pound lightly with the pestle. Heat the oil in a small frying pan until smoking and pour onto the mixture. Once the sizzling stops, combine lightly with the pestle and leave to infuse for a few minutes.

6. To make the dressing, mix the sesame oil and soy sauce with 60ml chicken stock. If you have any remaining chicken stock, season it and add a few spring onion slices. This can be served as a light broth to accompany the meal.

7. Slice the chicken Chinese-style and pour the dressing over it. Scatter with a little coriander and serve with the rice, condiments, broth and cucumber slices.

Prawn sambal is one of those dishes that I order whenever I find it on a menu. There is something about the sweet and sour nature of the tamarind sambal that works perfectly with firm seafood such as prawns or squid. Other seafood, or even chicken, can be substituted for the prawns.

Prawn sambal

Serves: 2
Preparation: 15 minutes
Cooking: 5 minutes

2 tsp neutral-flavoured oil
1 large brown onion, sliced
12 large prawns, peeled and deveined, tails intact
1 cup sambal assam (Pantry, page 23)

1. Heat the oil in a wok over medium-high heat until smoking and fry the onion for 2 minutes or until softened but not browned. Add the prawns and stir-fry for about 1 minute or until starting to turn opaque.

2. Add the sambal assam to the wok and simmer for 2–3 minutes until the prawns are cooked through. Serve with rice or, even better, as part of a dish of nasi lemak.

This is a bit of a Chinese restaurant classic. Crispy fried beef is served in a sweet citrus-flavoured sauce. While many restaurant versions are overly sweet and flavoured with orange juice, this version remains traditional with the uniquely piquant flavour of dried tangerine peel.

Crispy beef with shredded carrot

Serves: 2 as part of a shared meal
Preparation: 20 minutes
Cooking: 30 minutes + overnight refrigeration

200g rump steak, thinly sliced into 5mm strips
2 tbsp bicarbonate of soda
50g carrot, julienned
vegetable oil, to deep-fry

Marinade
2 tbsp cornflour
1 egg white, lightly beaten
1 tbsp Shaoxing wine

Sauce
2 pieces dried tangerine or orange peel
2 tbsp aromatic master stock (Pantry, page 18)
1 tsp chilli and garlic oil (Pantry, page 19)
1 tsp grated ginger
2 tsp Shaoxing wine
1½ tbsp rice wine vinegar
1 tsp light soy sauce
1 tsp dark soy sauce
1 tbsp caster sugar
1 tsp sesame oil
1 tsp cornflour

1. Place the beef in a glass or ceramic dish and coat with the bicarbonate of soda. Cover and leave in the fridge overnight to tenderise. Rinse off the bicarbonate of soda and pat the beef dry. Combine the beef with the marinade ingredients and set aside.

2. To make the sauce, soak the tangerine peel in boiling water for 20 minutes to soften, then finely chop. Mix with the remaining ingredients.

3. Half-fill a saucepan with oil and heat to 160°C. Deep-fry the beef in 3 batches for 8–10 minutes each batch until crispy and dark brown. Separate the strands of beef with tongs or chopsticks as they cook so that they don't clump together. Drain on paper towel.

4. Heat a wok over medium-high heat and add the sauce. Cook for 1 minute until slightly thickened and then add the beef and carrot. Toss for 1 minute until the beef is coated in sauce and the carrot has softened.

Siew yuk translates to 'roast pork' and I have to admit that it is possibly my greatest weakness. I can hardly walk through Chinatown without picking up a package to devour on the way home. The chilli and coriander relish is not traditional, but its tang counteracts the fattiness of the pork well. I have served this to my grandmother many times and the combination comes to you with her ringing endorsement (which is no small thing).

Siew yuk with chilli and coriander relish

Serves: 8 as part of a shared meal
Preparation: 20 minutes
Cooking: 1 hour 10 minutes + overnight marinating

1kg piece pork belly
1 tsp white peppercorns
8 garlic cloves
1 tbsp sea salt flakes

Chilli and coriander relish
1 tbsp finely chopped red birds-eye chilli
1 tbsp finely chopped coriander roots, stalks
  and leaves
2 garlic cloves, finely chopped
1 tbsp rice wine vinegar
1 tbsp light soy sauce
1 tsp caster sugar

1. Using a disposable razor without a lubricating strip, shave any hairs from the pork belly and trim away any undesirable parts. Put the pork in a colander and pour boiling water over the skin to blanch (you will see the skin tighten). Dry the pork well and poke lots of holes in the skin with a very sharp small knife. The more holes you poke, the better your crackling will be (I make hundreds of holes). Turn the pork over and score cuts into the meat side at 2–3cm intervals across the grain, cutting down to the skin but not through it.

2. Grind the peppercorns to a powder with a mortar and pestle, then add the garlic and pound to a smooth paste. Rub the paste into the meat side only, getting well into all the score lines. Do not get any paste on the skin. Place the pork on a rack in a baking tray and rub the sea salt into the skin. Put the tray in the fridge and leave the pork to dry overnight, uncovered. Blot the skin dry with paper towel if moisture pools on it.

3. Preheat the oven to 220°C. Drain off any liquid pooled in the tray. Put the tray in the oven and roast the pork skin-side-down for 10 minutes. Reduce the oven to 200°C and roast for another 20 minutes. Turn skin-side-up and roast for 30–40 minutes until the pork is cooked through.

4. Switch the oven to grill, open the door a crack to release steam and grill the pork for 3–5 minutes until the skin crackles.

5. Rest the pork for at least 15 minutes. Cut along the score lines and then across at 2–3cm intervals to make bite-sized pieces of pork.

6. To make the chilli and coriander relish, stir all the ingredients in a small bowl until the sugar has dissolved. Adjust the seasoning with a little salt, chilli or caster sugar if needed. Serve the pork with chilli and coriander relish.

Japanese potato salad is fluffy and creamy with a consistency more similar to rough mash than to a Western potato salad. It's ideal picnic food and, like most Japanese salads, is best eaten with chopsticks.

Japanese potato salad

Serves: 6
Preparation: 20 minutes
Cooking: about 30 minutes

4 large (about 650g) floury potatoes, such as Sebago
¼ tsp ground white pepper
½ small Lebanese cucumber
1 small white or brown onion, thinly sliced
½ small carrot
1 egg, at room temperature
1 cup Kewpie mayonnaise

1. Peel the potatoes and cut into 3cm cubes. Boil in salted water for 15 minutes or until quite tender. Drain and return the potatoes to the hot pan. Stir regularly over very low heat for 2–3 minutes to dry the potatoes without burning.

2. Transfer the potatoes to a deep bowl and season with a little salt and white pepper. Using a wooden spoon, crush the potatoes against the bowl to make a rough mash. Whip the potatoes vigorously with a wooden spoon for a few minutes until fluffy. Leave to cool to room temperature.

3. Meanwhile, peel the cucumber, leaving on a little peel for colour and texture. Cut in half lengthways and scoop out the seeds. Slice very thinly into half moons. Combine the cucumber and onion and toss with a little salt. Put in a colander and leave to drain for 15 minutes. Rinse off the salt under running water and dry on paper towel.

4. Peel the carrot and thinly slice into half moons. Boil in salted water for 3–5 minutes until tender. Drain and set aside on paper towel to cool.

5. Bring a small pan of water to the boil. Add the egg and boil for 8 minutes, then transfer the egg to iced water to stop the cooking process. When the egg is cool, peel and roughly chop.

6. Add the mayonnaise, carrot, cucumber and onion to the potato and whip vigorously with a wooden spoon. Stir in the egg. Serve at room temperature (as I prefer) or chilled.

The bitter melon, goya, is shaped like a fat, knobbly cucumber. Its strong, bitter flavour can be off-putting to some but in recent years I have come to love it. Like goya, pork has long been a staple of Okinawan cuisine but the occupation by US troops introduced new ingredients from military provisions. The arrival of SPAM gave this dish a whole new perspective. Chanpuru is the Okinawan term for a mixture and I was at first very hesitant about a stir-fry containing luncheon meat — but there's no point in being a snob about food when it tastes this good.

Goya chanpuru

Serves: 4
Preparation: 15 minutes
Cooking: 30 minutes + 30 minutes standing

150g firm tofu
½ large bitter melon
½ tsp sea salt flakes
1 tsp neutral-flavoured oil
100g SPAM luncheon meat, cut into small slices
½ brown onion, sliced
2 garlic cloves, crushed
100g pork shoulder or pork fillet, thinly sliced
100g shimeji mushrooms, gently separated
60ml mentsuyu (Pantry, page 26)
1 tbsp light soy sauce
2 eggs, beaten
75g bean sprouts
3 tsp bonito flakes, to serve

1. Wrap the tofu in paper towel and put a plate on top to compress. Leave for 30 minutes to drain (to prevent the tofu falling apart during cooking). Meanwhile, cut the bitter melon in half and scoop out the seeds with a spoon. Slice the melon into half moons and toss in the salt. Leave to drain in a colander for 20 minutes.

2. Unwrap the tofu and cut into pieces roughly the same size as the SPAM. Rinse the salt from the melon and dry on paper towels.

3. Heat the oil in a wok over medium heat until smoking. Add the SPAM and stir-fry until coloured on all sides, then remove with a slotted spoon. Add the tofu to the wok and toss gently until coloured on all sides. Lift out and drain on paper towel.

4. Add the onion and garlic to the wok, adding more oil if necessary, and stir-fry for 2 minutes until softened. Add the pork shoulder and stir-fry for 2 minutes until browned. Add the melon, mushrooms, mentsuyu and soy sauce. Stir-fry for 1–2 minutes until the melon and mushrooms soften and then add the SPAM and tofu. Stir to combine and move everything over to one side of the wok. Pour the eggs into the empty side of the wok and leave to set slightly. Fold the egg over itself a few times, then break into pieces and mix with the rest of the stir-fried ingredients. Add the bean sprouts and cook for 30 seconds until softened.

5. Transfer the stir-fry to a serving plate and top with the bonito flakes. The heat from the stir-fry will cause the bonito flakes to 'dance' on top of the stir-fry so add them just before bringing the dish to the table.

The most famous of Okinawa's wonderful pork dishes is Rafute. This simmered pork belly uses the local rice wine, awamori, named for the bubbles created by the rice moulds during fermentation. While sake is a reasonable substitute for awamori, I find a 2:1 mixture of sake and whisky gives the most faithful result. Don't be afraid of the fat here. The long cooking gives it a nice gelatinous texture and you can console yourself with the fact that Okinawans have the longest life expectancy on earth.

Rafute

Serves: 4 as part of a shared meal
Preparation: 15 minutes
Cooking: 2 hours 40 minutes

500g piece boneless pork belly
250ml awamori (or 160ml sake and 80ml whisky)
125ml dark soy sauce
110g caster sugar
125ml mirin
250ml ichiban dashi (Pantry, page 15)
6 thin slices ginger
1 leek
hot English mustard and steamed greens, to serve

1. Place the pork belly in a saucepan with plenty of cold water. Bring to the boil, then pour off the water. Run more cold water into the pan with the pork, making sure it is completely submerged. Bring to the boil again, then reduce the heat to a simmer. Partially cover the pan and simmer for 1 hour.

2. Remove the pork from the poaching water, keeping 250ml of the water. Cut the pork into pieces about 7cm long and 3–4 cm wide.

3. Put the pork poaching water, awamori, soy sauce, sugar, mirin, ichiban dashi and ginger in a small saucepan and add the pork pieces (they should be completely covered). Bring to the boil, then reduce the heat to a simmer. Cover the surface with a cartouche to ensure the pork remains submerged and simmer for 1½ hours until the pork is meltingly tender but still holds its shape. Remove the cartouche and the pork and simmer the liquid for 10 minutes until the sauce reduces slightly and becomes glossy.

4. Meanwhile, trim away the tough outer layers of the leek and cut in half lengthways. Finely shred and put into iced water to curl.

5. Serve cubes of pork with a good amount of sauce spooned over the top. Garnish with a smear of mustard and a small pile of greens. Top with the curled leeks.

Note: *A cartouche is a round of baking paper, cut to fit neatly and sit on the surface of the food as it cooks.*

The variety of yakitori dishes in Japan can make you wonder how many ways there are to prepare a bird as simple as chicken. Here are just five basic skewers but volumes could be written on yakitori. Aside from the flavour, I love yakitori for its sustainability and simplicity: all parts of the bird are used. It is a mark of respect to the bird and the farmer that, with just a few other ingredients, this simple bird can become a lavish feast. The quantities here make about six of each skewer, but if you are using a whole bird just make what you can from whatever meat you have.

Yakitori moriawase

Makes: about 36 skewers
Preparation: 30 minutes
Cooking: 35 minutes

250ml yakitori tare (Pantry, page 27)
shichimi togarashi (Japanese seven-spice pepper)
    and/or sansho powder (a Japanese powder similar
    in flavour to Sichuan pepper), to serve

Momo (chicken thigh skewers)
250g chicken thigh fillets

Negima (chicken and leek skewers)
200g chicken thigh fillets
2 slender baby leeks

Tsukune (chicken meatball skewers)
¼ brown onion, grated or processed to a purée
300g chicken meat from thighs and/or drumsticks,
    minced
1 egg yolk
1 tbsp cornflour
1 tsp grated ginger
½ sea salt flakes
20g chicken cartilage, finely chopped (optional)

Tebasaki (chicken wing skewers)
6 chicken wings

Kashiwa (chicken breast and thigh skewers)
125g chicken thigh fillet
125g chicken breast fillet
1 tsp grated fresh wasabi (a good substitute is
    powdered wasabi mixed with finely grated
    daikon radish instead of water)

1. For all yakitori, soak small bamboo skewers in water for at least 20 minutes before use (so they do not scorch). If you are grilling over a barbecue, yakitori grill or grill pan, cook over medium heat. If using an overhead grill, cook at high heat. Serve all the skewers together, with shichimi togarashi and/or sansho powder on the side.

2. To make momo, cut the chicken (across any sinew) into 3cm cubes. Thread onto skewers, squeezing with the palm of your hand to hold the meat tightly to the skewer. Grill for a few minutes, turning frequently, until just cooked on the outside. Baste with the yakitori tare and cook, basting occasionally, for a further 4 minutes until the chicken is cooked through.

3. To make negima, cut the chicken (across any sinew) into 3cm cubes. Cut the leeks into 5cm lengths. Thread the chicken and leek alternately onto skewers. Grill as for the momo, basting with yakitori tare.

4. To make tsukune, mix the onion, chicken mince, egg yolk, cornflour, ginger and salt. If the mince is too coarse, pulse in a food processor until smoother. Leave the chicken mixture to rest for 10 minutes in the fridge. Roll into 18–20 small balls and refrigerate for 10 minutes. Drop the balls a few at a time into boiling water and boil for 3 minutes until cooked through. Cool slightly, then refrigerate for 15 minutes until chilled. Thread the meatballs onto skewers (about 3 per skewer). Grill, turning occasionally, for about 3 minutes until charred, basting with yakitori tare as above.

5. To make tebasaki, remove the wing tips and separate the drumettes and wingettes (mid-joint). Split each wingette along the inside and fold out the meat to nearly expose the two inner bones. Insert the skewer underneath the bones to form a cross. While this wingette is the only part used in traditional yakitori, I also use the drumette split to the bone in the same way and threaded onto the same skewer. Season well with salt and grill, turning occasionally, for 5–8 minutes until cooked through. You can baste with yakitori tare, but I prefer this grilled simply with salt.

6. To make the kashiwa, cut the thigh and breast (across any sinew) into 3cm cubes. Thread onto skewers, alternating thigh and breast. Season with salt and grill, turning occasionally, for 4–6 minutes until just cooked through. The kashiwa can be basted with yakitori tare but I grill it with salt and serve with a little wasabi smeared on top.

My Aunty Chin makes a mean fish-head curry. The succulent meat from around the fish head is too good to be consigned to stock or, even worse, the bin. The strong of heart and stomach can reach for the eye, which is sometimes considered a delicacy, but is more often simply a test of bravado.

Aunty Chin's fish-head curry

Serves: 4
Preparation: 30 minutes
Cooking: 20 minutes + 20 minutes standing

1.5kg large white fish head (eg snapper, grouper or
   kingfish), anterior cut (see Note)
3 tbsp tamarind pulp
3 large brown onions, roughly chopped
3 garlic cloves, roughly chopped
5 red birds-eye chillies, split lengthways, seeds
   removed
2 tbsp neutral-flavoured oil
1 tbsp grated ginger
1 large handful curry leaves
250g okra, stalks trimmed
½ pineapple, peeled, cored and cut into 2cm cubes
2 tomatoes, cored and quartered
270ml can coconut cream
3 tsp fish sauce
¼ tsp salt
1 tsp caster sugar
juice of ½ lemon
cooked rice, to serve

Fish curry powder
5 tsp ground coriander
3 tsp ground cumin
1 tsp ground turmeric
1 tsp chilli powder
½ tsp white pepper

1. To make the fish curry powder, mix together all the ingredients in a bowl.

2. Rub the fish head with 1 tablespoon of the fish curry powder and set aside. Place the tamarind in a heatproof bowl and add 500ml hot water. Leave for 15 minutes, then squeeze out and keep all the liquid from the tamarind. Mix the onion, garlic and chilli in a food processor to a smooth paste.

3. Heat the oil in a wok until smoking and sear the fish head on both sides until lightly browned. Remove and set aside. Add the ginger to the wok and toss in the hot oil. Add the remaining curry powder and the curry leaves to the wok and toss for a few seconds until very fragrant. Add the onion, garlic and chilli paste and fry until the oil separates from the paste.

4. Add the okra to the wok and fry for 2 minutes until slightly softened. Add the pineapple and tomatoes and cook for 3 minutes. Add the coconut cream, tamarind liquid, fish sauce, salt and sugar and bring to the boil. Return the fish head to the wok and cover with sauce. Bring to the boil again, then immediately turn off the heat and cover the wok. Leave for 20 minutes for the fish to cook through. Add the lemon juice and serve with rice.

Note: *An anterior-cut fish head, cut straight down behind the gills, will hold plenty of tasty meat for this dish. Use 600g fish fillets instead of the head, if you prefer.*

Char kway teow is a great hawker-style noodle dish. It can also be made with any meat or poultry or simply left vegetarian. The secret to the characteristic charred flavour of this dish is to cook one portion at a time in the wok. Overloading the wok will braise or stew the noodles rather than fry them. If you like to entertain casually in your kitchen as I do, this is a great dish for groups of people with different tastes — have your seafood, chicken or meat ready to go and each guest can 'order' from the cook as their turn comes.

Seafood char kway teow

Serves: 1
Preparation: 10 minutes
Cooking: 20 minutes

2 fried fishcakes, sliced
1 tbsp neutral-flavoured oil
3 prawns, peeled and deveined
50g squid, sliced
1 garlic clove, finely chopped
40g Chinese spinach, chopped
1 spring onion, cut into 4cm lengths
1 egg
200g fresh thick, flat, white rice noodles
1 tbsp chicken stock or everyday soup
    stock (Pantry, page 14)
1 tsp light soy sauce
1 pinch chilli powder
¼ tsp salt
1 pinch white pepper
1 tsp Cheong Chan cooking caramel
50g bean sprouts
coriander, lemon wedges, chilli and garlic oil
    (Pantry, page 19) or chilli sauce, to serve

1. Boil the fishcake slices in water for 2 minutes until cooked. Drain and set aside.

2. Heat the oil over high heat in a large wok until smoking. Add the prawns, squid and fishcake slices. Stir-fry for about 2 minutes until almost cooked and then add the garlic, spinach and spring onion.

3. Push everything to one side of the wok and crack the egg into the space you have made. Break up the egg and mix everything together.

4. Add the noodles and toss to coat in the oil. Add the chicken stock, soy sauce, chilli powder, salt and pepper and then the cooking caramel. Stir-fry together, then add the bean sprouts and cook for just a few seconds (the bean sprouts will continue to cook in the heat from the noodles, and you want them to have a bit of crunch).

5. Serve with fresh coriander, a lemon wedge and some chilli and garlic oil or chilli sauce. If you're cooking for one, then sit down and enjoy it. Otherwise, take the next order and keep going until everyone is stuffed to the brim.

Larb are brilliant Thai and Laotian meat salads that have great texture. The secret lies in the ground rice powder that coats the meat — it adds texture and absorbs the flavour of the dressing. For these salads I prefer to mince the meat myself with a knife (rather than using a mincer or buying ready-made mince), as a coarser mince gives a more succulent result.

Larb duck

Serves: 2 as part of a shared meal
Preparation: 15 minutes
Cooking: 7 minutes + 15 minutes cooling

1 tbsp jasmine rice
2 tbsp everyday soup stock (Pantry, page 14) or water
120g duck breast, skin removed (see Note) and flesh
    roughly minced
2 eschalots, finely sliced (or ½ red onion, finely sliced)
1 kaffir lime leaf, shredded
1 stalk lemongrass, outer leaves discarded and inner
    core finely sliced
1 spring onion, finely sliced
1 tbsp fish sauce
1 tbsp lime juice
½ tsp chilli powder
1 pinch caster sugar
Chinese cabbage, coriander and Vietnamese mint,
    to serve

1. Heat a wok and add the jasmine rice. Toss over medium–high heat for about 5 minutes until the rice is well toasted and opaque. Cool, then grind to a rough powder with a mortar and pestle.

2. Put the stock or water in a small saucepan and bring to the boil. Add the duck breast and cook, stirring, over medium heat for about 2 minutes until the duck is just cooked and the liquid has evaporated. Remove from the heat. When the duck has stopped steaming, put in a metal bowl in the fridge to cool to room temperature. (Cooling the duck in the fridge accelerates the process and gives any potential bacteria less time to develop: important for a salad that will be served at room temperature.)

3. Add the eschalots, lime leaf, lemongrass, spring onion, fish sauce, lime juice, chilli powder and sugar to the cooled duck and mix well. Stir in the toasted rice powder. If the seasoning needs adjusting, add more lime juice or fish sauce. Leave for a few minutes for the flavours to combine before serving at room temperature. Serve on raw Chinese cabbage leaves and garnish with a little chopped coriander and Vietnamese mint.

Note: *I don't like to see the skin of the duck breast go to waste and, besides, salty crispy skin makes a great addition to this dish. Score the fat-side of the skin in a diamond pattern and salt it well on both sides. Heat 1 tsp oil in a small frying pan over medium heat. Add the duck skin, skin-side-down, and immediately put the base of another pan on top and press down firmly so the skin remains flat and in contact with the heat. Turn the skin after about 2 minutes and press down again to let the fat-side render into the pan. After 2 minutes turn the skin again so that it browns and crisps. Drain well, chop the skin into small pieces and scatter over the salad. It's not traditional, but it is delicious.*

This simple vegetable dish is a Malaysian classic. Just mention it to any Malaysian expat and wait for the knowing smile to come to their lips. Kangkong (water spinach or morning glory) was a very popular crop around Malaysia and Singapore after the Second World War. The hot and salty flavours of the chilli and belacan accentuate the unique texture of the vegetable. If kangkong is not available, try the same method with another vegetable such as broccoli, okra or even eggplant.

Belacan kangkong

Serves: 4 as part of a shared meal
Preparation: 15 minutes + 20 minutes soaking
Cooking: about 5 minutes

1 bunch kangkong (water spinach)
2 tbsp dried shrimp
2 tsp belacan (dried shrimp paste)
3 eschalots, sliced
2 garlic cloves, sliced
4 red birds-eye chillies, sliced
1 tbsp neutral-flavoured oil
3 tbsp everyday soup stock (Pantry, page 14) or chicken stock
¼ tsp sugar

1. Wash the kangkong well, trim off any woody ends and cut into 10cm lengths. If any stalks are especially thick, split them in half lengthways. Soak in water until ready to use. Meanwhile, soak the dried shrimp in hot water for 20 minutes and then drain.

2. Pound the dried shrimp, belacan, eschalots, garlic and chillies to a rough paste with a mortar and pestle.

3. Heat the oil in a wok and add the paste. Stir-fry over medium heat for 1–2 minutes until darkened and fragrant. Shake any excess water from the kangkong and add to the wok. Stir fry for 2–3 minutes until the kangkong begins to soften. Add the stock and sugar, toss through and cook for 30 seconds. Taste the liquid from the bottom of the wok and season with salt if necessary.

Katsudon is a Japanese favourite — a rice bowl of a crispy pork cutlet coated in a semi-set egg sauce and served over rice. Mitsuba (trefoil) is the perfect garnish for this dish, but it is often difficult to find outside Japan, so as an acceptable substitute use snow pea shoots.

Katsudon

Serves: 2
Preparation: 20 minutes
Cooking: about 10 minutes

75g plain flour

1 tsp sea salt flakes

2 thick pork cutlets (about 180g each), deboned

3 eggs, lightly beaten

100g panko breadcrumbs

vegetable oil, to deep-fry

250ml mentsuyu (Pantry, page 26)

½ small brown onion, sliced

3 eggs, extra

3 cups cooked Japanese short-grain rice and mitsuba (trefoil) or snow pea shoots, to serve

1. Mix together the flour and salt and dip each cutlet in seasoned flour, then egg, then back into flour and then back into egg before coating with panko breadcrumbs. Press the crumbs on gently and shake off any excess. This double layer of egg and flour gives a deliciously thick coating to the cutlet.

2. Half-fill a saucepan or wok with oil and heat to 160°C. Cook the cutlets for 5–6 minutes, or until just cooked and succulent inside and crispy golden brown outside. Set aside to rest.

3. Combine the mentsuyu and onion in a small frying pan. Simmer for 3 minutes until the onion softens and becomes translucent. Add a little more mentsuyu if it becomes too dry. Loosely whisk the 3 extra eggs so that the yolks are broken but the yolks and whites are not totally combined.

4. Thickly slice the cutlets (take care the crust doesn't come away) and add to the pan. Pour in the egg mixture, cover the pan with a lid and simmer for 30 seconds. Turn off the heat and leave for 1 minute so that the egg is loosely set. Shuffle the pan occasionally so that the egg doesn't stick to it.

5. Spoon cooked rice into two serving bowls. Slide the cutlets and egg onto the rice and top with mitsuba or snow pea shoots.

While this may look a tricky list of ingredients, all are usually available from your local Chinese grocery. Bah kuh teh translates as 'pork bone tea' and the pungent Chinese medicinal herbs give this a unique and inviting aroma.

Bah kuh teh

Serves: 4–6
Preparation: 30 minutes
Cooking: 2 hours 20 minutes

2 whole heads garlic
1 kg pork belly (or pork spare ribs)
500g pork ribs (about 2 racks)
2 tsp salt
1 tbsp caster sugar
3 tbsp light soy sauce
50g dried shiitake mushrooms
5 fried tofu puffs, halved
10g goji berries (juzi)
chopped coriander and spring onions, to serve
3 sticks youtiao (Chinese fried bread), sliced, to serve
cooked rice, to serve
3 sliced birds-eye chillies mixed with dark soy sauce, to serve

Herb and spice bag
20g codonopsis pilosula root (tang shen)
20g dried Chinese angelica (dang gui)
10g lovage root (chuan xiong)
20g rehmannia glutinosa (shu di)
5 slices licorice root (gan cao)
20g Solomon's seal root (yu zhu)
2 pieces dried tangerine peel
15g cassia bark
6g star anise
5g white peppercorns

1. For the herb and spice bag, briefly rinse all the ingredients and wrap in a large square of muslin. Gather the ends at the top and tie with string to form a pouch.

2. Pour 3.5 litres of cold water into a very large pot (preferably a claypot), add the herb and spice bag and garlic and bring to the boil. Simmer, covered, for 30 minutes. Meanwhile, put the pork belly and ribs in another large pot and cover with cold water. Bring to the boil, then remove the pork belly and ribs and add them to the boiling soup stock with the salt, sugar and soy sauce. Simmer, covered, for 1½ hours until the pork is very tender, skimming occasionally to remove any fat or scum.

3. Meanwhile, soak the shiitake mushrooms in hot water for 30 minutes until softened. Discard the woody stems.

4. Remove the pork from the soup, set aside to cool, then slice. Add the shiitake mushrooms, tofu puffs and goji berries to the soup and boil for 20 minutes. Remove the herb and spice bag. Taste and adjust the seasoning if necessary with salt and sugar.

5. To serve, put sliced pork and ribs in a bowl and cover with hot soup, making sure to serve some mushrooms and tofu in with the soup. Scatter with spring onion and coriander and serve with youtiao, rice and chillies in soy sauce. (I like to dunk the youtiao in the soup and eat with the pork, chilli and rice in a big mouthful.)

Chirashi zushi translates as 'scattered sushi'. Sweet and flavoursome ingredients and condiments are scattered over sushi rice to give a simple and delicious dish.

Chirashi zushi

Serves: 2
Preparation: 30 minutes + standing
Cooking time: about 30 minutes

100g snow peas
1 sheet nori
3 cups cooked sushi rice (On sushi, page 34), at
    room temperature
3 tbsp white sesame seeds, toasted

Seasoned prawns
10 prawns, peeled and deveined
125ml ichiban dashi (Pantry, page 15)
2 tbsp rice wine vinegar
1 tbsp caster sugar
1 tsp soy sauce

Shiitake mushrooms
10 dried shiitake mushrooms
125ml ichiban dashi
1½ tbsp caster sugar
1 tbsp sake
2 tbsp mirin
2 tbsp light soy sauce

Kinishi tamago
2 eggs
1 tsp caster sugar
1 tsp neutral-flavoured oil

Carrot
1 small carrot
125ml ichiban dashi
1 tsp vinegar
1 tsp caster sugar

Seasoned lotus root
50g lotus root
juice of ½ lemon
2 tbsp ichiban dashi
2 tbsp rice wine vinegar
1 tbsp caster sugar
¼ tsp salt

1. For the seasoned prawns, poach the prawns in simmering salted water for 3–5 minutes until cooked through. Mix together the dashi, vinegar, sugar and soy and stir until the sugar has dissolved. Drain the prawns, add to the seasoning mixture and leave to season for 30 minutes in the fridge. Drain the prawns and set aside.

2. To prepare the shiitake mushrooms, rinse the mushrooms and place in a heatproof bowl. Pour on boiling water and leave to soak for 30 minutes. Discard the woody stalks and slice the caps thinly. Put in a small saucepan with the dashi, sugar, sake, mirin and soy and simmer for 10 minutes, until all the liquid has evaporated. Leave to cool.

3. For the kinishi tamago, break the egg yolks with chopsticks or a fork and mix gently with the whites (do not whisk or there will be too much air in the mixture). Pass through a sieve, then mix in the sugar and a pinch of salt. Heat a small frying pan over medium heat, brush with a little oil and pour in a little of the egg, tilting the pan to make a very thin omelette. When just set, flip over and heat until cooked through but not browned. Drain on paper towel. Cook the rest of the omelettes (about 3) then roll up each one and slice thinly.

4. To prepare the carrot, peel and cut into 5mm-thick rounds. If you have a cutter, you could cut each round into a decorative shape. Bring the dashi, vinegar, sugar and a pinch of salt to the boil in a small saucepan and add the carrot. Simmer for 4–5 minutes until the liquid has evaporated. Cool the carrot to room temperature.

5. To make the seasoned lotus root, peel the lotus root and thinly slice. Soak in water with lemon juice for 5 minutes and then blanch in boiling salted water for 2–3 minutes. Mix together the dashi, vinegar, sugar and salt, stirring to dissolve the sugar, and add the lotus root. Leave for 30 minutes, then drain and set aside.

6. Blanch the snow peas in boiling salted water for 1–2 minutes, drain, then plunge into iced water. Drain again, pat dry with paper towel and then thinly slice on an angle. Toast the nori over an open flame or under a grill and crumble into small pieces.

7. To assemble chirashi zushi, put the rice in a large bamboo basin or bowl. Add the sesame seeds, nori, mushrooms, carrots and snow peas. Mix well and then arrange on a serving dish. Scatter with the prawns, lotus root and kinishi tamago.

This shows an interesting Japanese seasoning technique, which is to place cooked food into a liquid to steep. Strange to Western tastes is the use of this technique with fried food, which loses much of its crispiness but absorbs the flavour of the seasoning liquid with delicious results. Nanbanzuke roughly translates to 'Southern barbarian style' and refers to the Portuguese background of the dish — it is based on the classic Portuguese escabeche, which was also a precursor to the now-ubiquitous tempura.

Chicken nanbanzuke

Serves: 2 as part of a shared meal
Preparation: 15 minutes
Cooking: 6 minutes + 1 hour standing

200g chicken thigh fillets
1 tbsp plain flour
½ tsp sea salt flakes
1 pinch ground white pepper
vegetable oil, for deep-frying
½ leek, white part only, julienned
½ small carrot, julienned
½ stalk celery, julienned

Seasoning liquid
100ml ichiban dashi (Pantry, page 15)
150ml rice wine vinegar
1 tbsp caster sugar
½ tsp salt
¼ tsp ground white pepper
1 tbsp light soy sauce
3 small dried chillies, chopped (or ¼ tsp dried chilli flakes)

1. To make the seasoning liquid, put all the ingredients in a saucepan and stir over low heat until the sugar has dissolved. Pour the seasoning liquid into a shallow dish and leave to cool.

2. Slice the chicken into thin strips and coat in the combined flour, salt and pepper. Half-fill a medium saucepan with vegetable oil and heat to 180°C. Deep-fry the chicken in 2 batches for 3–5 minutes until deep golden brown and just cooked through, separating the strips with chopsticks or tongs during frying to prevent them sticking together. Lift the chicken out of the oil with a slotted spoon and plunge immediately into the seasoning liquid (the chicken will sizzle).

3. When all the chicken is in the seasoning liquid, scatter with the leek, carrot and celery. Leave for 30 minutes, then toss and leave for another 30 minutes.

4. To serve, arrange the chicken and vegetables on a plate and pour on just a little of the seasoning liquid. Serve at room temperature.

I make this simple, healthy cucumber salad almost every day in summer. The refreshing coolness of the cucumber and salty tang of the salt, sesame and nori are a perfect match. Make sure the cucumbers are well chilled and use the best-quality salt you have.

Bashed cucumbers

Serves: 4
Preparation: 15 minutes
Cooking: 2 minutes

4 Lebanese cucumbers or 1 large continental
    cucumber, chilled
1 tbsp sesame oil
1 tbsp ice-cold water
½ tsp sea salt flakes
¼ sheet dried nori (optional)
½ tsp mixed black and white sesame seeds (optional)
½ tsp bonito flakes (optional)

1. Chill a metal bowl in the fridge for a few minutes. Peel the cucumbers in strips, leaving on a little of the skin for texture and colour. Wrap the cucumbers tightly in a clean tea towel and bash with a rolling pin or mallet until cracked and broken into shards. If necessary, break them apart further with your hands. Put in the chilled bowl.

2. Sprinkle the sesame oil, water and salt over the cucumbers, toss well and put in the fridge for just a few minutes for the salt and cucumbers to get to know each other. You can serve this as it is now or top with a few of these other ingredients.

3. Toast the nori by holding it over a naked flame with tongs until it is brittle. Let it cool slightly and then break it apart with your hands into a bowl. If you are using sesame seeds, toast in a dry frying pan over medium heat for about 2 minutes until the white seeds are golden and fragrant.

4. Transfer the cucumbers and a tablespoon or two of their dressing and juice to a serving dish and top with the nori, sesame seeds and bonito flakes.

Taco rice is an Okinawan dish that originated in the 1960s as a result of the post-war occupation by US troops. It combines the popular flavours of a taco with the Japanese concept of a rice bowl and is hugely popular with the Okinawa locals — Japanese and American alike. This is a delicious example of how the food and history of a culture are inextricably linked.

Taco rice

Serves: 2
Preparation: 20 minutes
Cooking: 30 minutes

2 tsp olive oil
300g beef mince
2 tsp light soy sauce
125 ml mentsuyu (Pantry, page 26)
2 cups shredded lettuce, to serve
1 cup grated cheddar cheese, to serve
3 cups cooked Japanese short-grain rice, to serve

Spice mix
½ tsp onion powder
¼ tsp garlic powder
¼ tsp chilli powder
¼ tsp ground cumin
¼ tsp dried oregano
½ tsp hot paprika
¼ tsp sea salt flakes
1 pinch ground black pepper

Fresh salsa
50g cherry tomatoes, quartered
2 tsp rice wine vinegar
¼ tsp caster sugar
¼ tsp sea salt flakes
2 tbsp chopped flat-leaf parsley
¼ red onion, sliced

1. To make the spice mix, combine all the ingredients and set aside.

2. Heat the oil in a medium saucepan over medium-high heat and brown the beef mince, breaking up any lumps with a wooden spoon as it cooks. Drain off any excess oil and return the mince to the pan. Add the spice mix, soy sauce and mentsuyu. Cover the surface with a cartouche and simmer for 20 minutes, stirring occasionally.

3. Meanwhile, to make the salsa, combine all the ingredients and leave in the fridge for 20 minutes to let the flavours develop.

4. To build the rice bowls, layer the rice evenly in the bowls. Layer the mince on top of the rice and top with the cheese. Scatter the lettuce around the bowl and top everything with fresh salsa. You can eat as it is or toss everything together first and then eat.

Note: *A cartouche is a round of baking paper, cut to fit neatly and sit on the surface of the food as it cooks to keep in moisture.*

Pork neck is an underrated cut of meat, but its fat content makes it perfect for roasted or barbecued dishes like this. Char siew ('grilled pork') is often seen hanging in the windows of Chinese barbecue shops, dyed red. I don't like to use too many colourings or preservatives in my cooking so I have left out the red colouring. If you prefer your char siew a more traditional colour, add red colouring.

Char siew pork neck

Serves: 4–6
Preparation: 25 minutes
Cooking: 40 minutes + 2 hours marinating

8 garlic cloves, roughly chopped
2 tbsp grated ginger
4 tbsp honey
2 tbsp caster sugar
2 tbsp Shaoxing wine
125ml soy sauce
1kg boneless pork neck, cut into 5cm-wide strips

Five-spice salt
3 star anise
12 cloves
2 cinnamon quills
1 tbsp fennel seeds
1 tbsp Sichuan peppercorns
2 tsp sea salt flakes

1. To make the five-spice salt, roast the spices and salt in a dry frying pan over medium heat for about 3 minutes until fragrant. Cool, grind to a powder with a mortar and pestle and transfer to a bowl.

2. Combine 1½ tbsp of five-spice salt with the garlic, ginger, honey, sugar, wine and soy in the mortar and grind to a loose paste. Put the pork neck in a non-metallic shallow dish, pour the loose paste over the top and leave to marinate in the fridge for at least 2 hours but preferably overnight.

3. Preheat the oven to 200°C. Transfer the pork and marinade to a roasting dish just big enough to hold the pork. Bake the pork for 10 minutes. Turn to coat with the reducing marinade and bake for 25–30 minutes until glazed and caramelised and just cooked through. (Alternatively, cook on a barbecue over medium heat.) Rest the pork for at least 10 minutes before slicing to serve.

Note: *You only need half the five-spice salt for this recipe. Keep the rest in an airtight container to use next time.*

Unlike sweet and sour pork, which has its origins in the traditional Cantonese sugar and vinegar pork, lemon chicken is a westernised dish that mirrors Cantonese flavours. Its creation is often credited to Lee Lum, the Cantonese chef at New York eatery Pearl's — a hotspot during the wild times of Studio 54. Lee Lum's recipe was published in **The New York Times Magazine** *in 1969 and has come to epitomise the American concept of Chinese food. This is my (rather more fresh and natural) version of a modern classic, without the MSG and lemon extract.*

Lemon chicken

Serves: 4 as part of a shared meal
Preparation: 25 minutes
Cooking: 10 minutes + 30 minutes marinating

2 chicken breast fillets
neutral-flavoured oil, to shallow-fry
2 egg whites
70g water chestnut flour (see Note)
finely shredded iceberg lettuce and cooked white rice,
   to serve

Marinade
1 tbsp light soy sauce
¼ tsp sesame oil
½ tsp sea salt flakes
1 tbsp Shaoxing wine

Sauce
3 tbsp caster sugar
60ml white vinegar
finely grated zest and juice of 1 lemon
125ml everyday soup stock (Pantry, page 14) or
   chicken stock
2 tsp arrowroot (tapioca starch) or cornflour
1 small carrot, julienned
3 spring onions, julienned

1. To make the marinade, combine all the ingredients in a small bowl or jug.

2. Place each chicken breast between 2 sheets of cling wrap and beat lightly to a uniform thickness of 1.5 to 2cm. Place in a shallow dish and add the marinade, turning to coat the chicken well. Leave in the fridge to marinate for 30 minutes.

3. Heat about 2cm oil in a large frying pan over medium heat. Beat the egg whites until fluid and frothy. If the water chestnut flour is caked and granular, pound it in a mortar to make a fine powder and then transfer to a plate or tray. Dip the chicken into the egg white, then into the flour. Fry for 3–4 minutes until golden brown, turn and fry for a further 3 minutes. Drain on paper towels.

4. To make the sauce, combine the sugar, vinegar, lemon zest and juice and stock in a wok over medium-low heat. Bring to a simmer, stirring to dissolve the sugar. Mix the arrowroot with a little cold water and stir into the sauce. Cook, stirring, for about 1 minute until the sauce is clear and glossy. Add the carrot and spring onion and cook for 30 seconds to soften.

5. Slice the chicken into 2.5cm strips and arrange over the shredded lettuce. Pour the sauce over the top and serve with rice.

Note: I have kept Lee Lum's secret ingredient of water chestnut flour, which gives the chicken an ultra-crisp coating that doesn't soften quickly in the rich sauce. If you can't find water chestnut flour, you can use cornflour instead, but the coating won't be quite as crisp.

This deceptively simple dish represents 600 years of political struggle, industry, war and romance. It tells the story of the powerful Malacca Sultanate, which ruled over that strategic Malaysian shipping port from the 15th century. In its very ingredients you can see the presence of indigenous Malays, the Hindu and Tamil influence of the Sultanate, and later Portuguese, Dutch and British colonial influences. Ayam Kapitan, or Captain's chicken, was named for the captains of the Chinese trading communities that lived and worked in Malacca in those times.

Ayam Kapitan

Serves: 4
Preparation: 25 minutes
Cooking: about 30 minutes

1 whole chicken (1.5kg), jointed
1 tbsp neutral-flavoured oil
5 eschalots, sliced
270ml can coconut cream
juice of ½ lime
2 kaffir lime leaves, finely shredded, to serve

Base paste
8 red birds-eye chillies, split, seeds removed
3 eschalots
5 cloves garlic
2.5cm each ginger, galangal and turmeric, peeled and sliced
5 candlenuts
2 stalks lemongrass, white part only
1 tsp belacan (dried shrimp paste)

1. To make the base paste, combine the ingredients in a food processor or use a mortar and pestle to grind to a smooth paste.

2. Trim any visible fat from the chicken. Heat the oil in a saucepan big enough to hold the chicken and fry the paste over medium heat for about 5 minutes until brown and fragrant. Add the eschalots and chicken, turning to coat in the paste. Fry for a further 2 minutes until the eschalots are softened.

3. Add the coconut cream with 100ml water and cover the pan with a lid. Bring to the boil, reduce the heat and simmer for 20 minutes. Uncover and simmer for 5–10 minutes until the chicken is tender and the sauce has reduced. Stir in the lime juice and scatter with lime leaves to serve.

This small cold dish is one of my favourite snacks — I regularly make huge portions of this and store it in the fridge for grazing purposes. The name kimpira is taken from the fabled Japanese hero Sakata Kimpira, about whom Joururi puppet plays were popular during the Edo period.

Kimpira

Serves: 2
Preparation: 15 minutes
Cooking: about 10 minutes

100g burdock (fresh or frozen)
juice of ½ lemon
75g carrot
1 tsp vegetable oil
1 dried red chilli
60ml sake
1 tbsp caster sugar
1 tbsp mirin
1 tbsp soy sauce
½ tsp toasted golden sesame seeds

1. To prepare the burdock, lightly scrub the skin to remove any dirt. There is no need to peel the burdock. Cut into 5cm lengths and then julienne. Soak in water with added lemon juice for 10 minutes, then rinse and drain. If you are using frozen burdock, thaw and julienne (if not already cut). Peel and julienne the carrot.

2. Heat the oil in a small saucepan and fry the burdock and carrot over medium heat for 1 minute. Add the chilli, sake, sugar, mirin and soy sauce and bring to a simmer. Reduce the heat to very low and simmer for 7–10 minutes until the liquid has completely evaporated. Tilt the pan over the heat towards the end of cooking to pool any remaining liquid to one side — this helps all the liquid evaporate without burning the contents of the pan.

3. Transfer the kimpira to a tray and cool to room temperature. Scatter with sesame seeds to serve.

Note: *Soaking the fresh burdock in acidulated water prevents discolouration.*

This a relatively modern Malaysian dish that only reaches back 20 years or so in history. While relatively young in tradition, the combination of toasted coconut, creamy butter and smoky curry leaves with the sweet prawns make it an instant classic.

Butter prawns

Serves: 4 as part of a shared meal
Preparation: 15 minutes
Cooking: 6 minutes

500g raw prawns, unpeeled
neutral-flavoured oil, to deep-fry
3 egg yolks, beaten
45g desiccated coconut
100g unsalted butter, roughly chopped
1 large handful curry leaves
8 red birds-eye chillies, finely chopped
2 garlic cloves, minced
1 tsp light soy sauce
½ tsp Shaoxing wine
1 pinch ground white pepper
¼ tsp sea salt flakes
2 tsp caster sugar
cooked rice, to serve

1. Cut each prawn through the back and remove the intestinal tract. Trim the legs. Half-fill a large wok with oil and heat to 180°C. Deep-fry the prawns in 2 batches for 2–3 minutes each batch until crispy. Set aside to drain on paper towels.

2. Pour the oil from the wok to leave 1 tablespoon. Pour the egg yolks into the wok through a sieve — as the egg enters the wok, whisk to form strands and clumps. Remove the egg from the wok and set aside.

3. Clean the wok and dry-fry the coconut until golden brown. Remove from the wok.

4. Melt the butter in the wok and fry the curry leaves for just a few seconds until glossy and crisping. Add the chillies and garlic and fry for 30 seconds until fragrant. Add the prawns, coconut, egg, soy sauce, wine, pepper, salt and sugar and cook for 1 minute until everything is combined. Serve immediately with rice and eat — prawn heads, shells and all.

This is my favourite Kuala Lumpur dish of all time (and in a city with so many delicious things to eat that is really saying something). Since I was a kid, my family's ritual has been to go out to eat these noodles on our first night in KL. There are three secrets to this dish: the rendered pork fat used to fry the noodles; the sticky black caramel sauce; and the crispy pork lardons that are scattered throughout. It's not much to look at, but it's heaven on a plate.

Black hokkien noodles

Serves: 4
Preparation: 15 minutes
Cooking: 1 hour 20 minutes

200g piece pork belly
2 tbsp neutral-flavoured oil
3 garlic cloves, finely chopped
½ tsp white peppercorns, ground
1 tbsp dark soy sauce
2 tsp cornflour
600g hokkien noodles
12 raw prawns, peeled and deveined, tails intact
100g squid tubes, scored and cut into triangles
60g shredded Chinese cabbage
125ml chicken stock or everyday soup stock
  (Pantry, page 14)
4 tbsp Cheong Chan cooking caramel
1 tsp caster sugar
chilli sauce or pickled chillies, to serve

1. Remove the skin from the pork and discard. Separate the fat from the meat and cut the fat into small lardons about 5mm wide. Heat the oil in a wok or small frying pan and render the lardons over extremely low heat, stirring occasionally, for about 1¼ hours. The liquid fat will separate and you will be left with small crisp lardons of pork fat (chu yau cha). Separate the lardons from the oil and keep both.

2. Chop the pork belly meat into small thin slivers and marinate in the combined garlic, pepper, soy sauce and cornflour. Separate the noodles in a large bowl of cold water, then drain.

3. Heat 2 tbsp of the reserved pork fat in the wok until hot and add the pork meat. Stir-fry over medium-high heat for about 3 minutes until brown. Add the prawns and squid and stir-fry for 30 seconds. Add the Chinese cabbage and toss for another 30 seconds.

4. Add the noodles and stock to the wok, then add the caramel sauce and sugar. Toss together and cook for 2 minutes until the noodles are cooked and a thick black gravy coats the entire dish. Spoon into bowls, scatter with crispy pork lardons and serve with a spoonful of your favourite chilli sauce or pickled chillies.

5. Don't get any on your shirt.

Kaya toast is a breakfast institution in Malaysia and Singapore. The region's Hainanese Chinese immigrants (from whom I am descended) are often considered a driving force of culinary innovation in modern Malaysian and Singaporean cuisine. They bridged the cultural divide between local cuisine, traditional Chinese recipes and the colonial classes for whom they worked as cooks and domestic help. Kaya toast is a variation on traditional British toast with jam, using the local coconut curd in place of Western preserve. This is my grandmother's recipe.

Kaya toast

Makes: 6½ cups kaya, which will keep for 1 month
Preparation: 40 minutes
Cooking: 50 minutes

white bread and salted butter, to serve

Kaya
10 free-range eggs
1kg caster sugar
5 pandan leaves, tied together in a knot
550ml coconut cream (see Note)
15g unsalted butter
50g caster sugar, extra

1. To make kaya, combine the eggs and sugar in a high bowl and stir with a whisk for about 30 minutes until extremely smooth. Stir only in one direction and be careful not to aerate the mixture — any air bubbles will affect the texture of the curd. Strain through a sieve into the top of a double boiler and add the pandan leaves.

2. Half-fill the base of the double boiler with water and bring to a simmer. (If you don't have a double boiler, make this in a glass bowl sitting over a pan of simmering water. The base of the bowl must not touch the water.) Place the upper section on top. Stir over low heat for 10 minutes to ensure all the sugar has dissolved. Strain the coconut cream through a fine sieve into the mixture and cook, stirring constantly in only one direction, for about 30 minutes or until the mixture thickens.

3. Combine the butter and extra sugar in a small saucepan and stir over medium-low heat until a rich, dark caramel forms. Add the caramel to the curd and continue stirring until combined. Wrap the lid of the double boiler in a tea towel and cover the top (to prevent water condensing and dripping into the curd). Cook for 5 minutes until thickened further. Discard the pandan leaves and transfer the kaya to sterilised jars to cool. As it cools it will thicken further. Cover tightly and store in the fridge for up to 1 month.

4. To make kaya toast, take 2 slices of good white bread and trim the crusts. Toast the bread and cover with a few thin (or thick!) slices of butter. Thickly spread one piece of toast with kaya and sandwich with another piece of toast. Cut into fingers and enjoy with a cup of kopi tiam or a regular coffee.

Note: *If you are using fresh coconut cream, you will need about 3 coconuts. Alternatively, skim off the rich, top layer from canned coconut cream, discarding any watery milk below — you'll need about three 400ml cans. You can halve the quantity if you like.*

*While the near-raw centre of the beef may seem
more suited to a fillet cut of beef, beef tataki works
well with any flavoursome cut that can be eaten
rare. Rump, tri-tip and sirloin are all good choices.*

Beef tataki

Serves: 2 as part of a shared meal
Preparation: 10 minutes
Cooking: about 8 minutes + 1 hour chilling

300g piece good-quality beef tri-tip or rump, about
    5cm thick
¼ tsp sea salt flakes
¼ tsp ground black pepper
2 tsp neutral-flavoured oil
1 tbsp light soy sauce
1 tbsp sake
½ tsp finely chopped chives
½ tsp grated garlic
½ tsp grated ginger

Ponzu dipping sauce
1½ tbsp lemon juice
1 tbsp light soy sauce

1. Trim any visible surface fat from the beef and rub
   with the salt and pepper. Heat the oil in a heavy
   based frying pan with a tight-fitting lid over high
   heat until the oil is smoking. Quickly sear the beef
   on all sides until well browned. Turn the heat to
   low and add the soy sauce and sake, rolling the
   beef through the sauce to coat well for about
   1 minute. Turn off the heat and put the lid on the
   pan. Leave for 5 minutes, then remove the beef.

2. Return the pan to the heat and simmer the liquid
   until reduced to about 1 tbsp. Pour over the beef
   and leave to rest for a further 1 minute. Transfer
   the beef to the fridge for about 1 hour to chill
   completely.

3. Slice the beef thinly across the grain and arrange
   on a serving plate. Top with mounds of chives,
   garlic and ginger. Mix together the lemon juice
   and light soy to make a ponzu dipping sauce and
   serve with the beef.

Freshly made tofu is simple to do at home and very different from the bought product. The addition of some simple and flavourful condiments takes this simple tofu and makes it a complete dish.

Zaru tofu

Serves: 4 as part of a shared meal
Preparation: 30 minutes
Cooking: about 15 minutes + overnight soaking

2 cups dried soy beans
15ml nigari (magnesium chloride solution)
chopped chives, grated ginger, bonito flakes,
    sesame seeds and best-quality salt, to serve

1. Soak the soy beans in plenty of water overnight and then drain. Measure out 2 litres fresh water. Transfer the soy beans in batches to a blender, add a little of the water and mix to a purée. Transfer each batch of purée to a large saucepan, rinsing the blender with a little more of the water to ensure all the purée is transferred to the pan.

2. Bring the purée and water to the boil and then immediately remove from the heat. Line a large colander with a double layer of muslin and place over another large pot. Pour the hot liquid through the muslin and gather the muslin around any residue. Twist the muslin and, with a wooden spoon, press down firmly on the residue to extract all the soy milk. Pour the soy milk into a large measuring jug and measure out 1.5 litres.

3. Mix the nigari with 125ml water (please note that different brands of nigari vary in concentration; some may not require further dilution with water. Follow the directions on your brand of nigari powder or solution).

4. Transfer 1.5 litres of soy milk back into the pot and bring to the boil. Simmer for 5 minutes, then remove from the heat. Add half the nigari mixture and gently stir once. Leave for 5 minutes, then add the remaining nigari mixture and gently stir once. Cover the pot and leave to sit for a further 5 minutes. Drain the whey from the curds and transfer the curds to a small sieve or tofu mold lined with a double layer of muslin. Twist the muslin to squeeze liquid from the tofu and place a weight on top of the tofu to maintain pressure and to keep the muslin in place.

5. After 3 minutes the tofu should have stopped dripping. Transfer the wrapped parcel to a basin of cold water and leave for 5 minutes. Remove the tofu from the water, drain for another 5 minutes, unwrap and place on a bamboo strainer. Let the tofu sit on the strainer for 5 minutes, then serve topped with the chives, ginger, bonito flakes, sesame seeds and salt.

Fire chicken certainly lives up to its name. It's scorchingly hot but, in fact, the hotter this dish is, the tastier it is. Four types of heat (chilli powder, black pepper, English mustard and fresh chilli) are layered with four types of sweetness (honey, sugar, bean paste and nashi pear) so that the flavours work in synergy. In Tokyo my Friday after-work unwind with friends would always start in Koreatown with a plate of fire chicken and an ice-cold beer.

Fire chicken (bul dak)

Serves: 4–6
Preparation: 30 minutes
Cooking: 25 minutes + 30 minutes marinating

1 whole chicken (1.5kg), cut into large pieces
1 tbsp neutral-flavoured oil
sliced spring onions, to serve

Marinade
2 tbsp sake or cheong ju (Korean rice wine)
1 tbsp soy sauce
1 tbsp neutral-flavoured oil
1 tbsp caster sugar
2 tbsp honey, rice malt syrup or mul yut (Korean malt syrup)
1 tsp ground black pepper

Sauce
3 tbsp chilli powder (preferably Korean)
1 tbsp kochujan (Korean chilli bean paste)
2 tbsp soy sauce
1 tbsp sesame oil
2 tbsp honey, rice malt syrup or mul yut (Korean malt syrup)
1 tbsp caster sugar
2 tsp hot English mustard
3-4 red birds-eye chillies (or more, if you can handle the heat)
3 garlic cloves
½ large brown onion, cut into chunks
½ large nashi pear, peeled and cut into chunks

1. To make the marinade, combine all the ingredients in a ceramic or glass dish. Combine the chicken with the marinade and leave in the fridge for 30 minutes.

2. To make the sauce, put all the ingredients into a small food processor and mix to a smooth purée.

3. Heat the oil in a large frying pan big enough to hold all the chicken. Fry the chicken all together over medium-low heat for about 5 minutes, turning to colour it evenly on all sides. The chicken will blacken quickly, as the sugar and honey from the marinade caramelise — don't be concerned; this adds to the flavour.

4. Reduce the heat to medium and cook the chicken for about 10 minutes or until half cooked. Stir in the sauce and cook for a further 5–10 minutes until the sauce darkens to deep red and the chicken is cooked through. Transfer to a plate and scatter with spring onion to serve.

Note: *I serve this with white pickled daikon (Pantry, page 15) and a simple coleslaw. To make coleslaw, swirl a big dollop of mayonnaise with kochujan (Korean chilli bean paste) and toss through finely shredded cabbage and white onion which has been shaved on a mandolin.*

Somen is a quintessential Japanese summer dish: light, fresh and cold. In Japan this is sometimes served as 'nagashi somen' — a long length of split bamboo is set up and people sit on either side as water flows down the bamboo, carrying somen. Each person has their own dipping sauce and catches the somen as it flows past them. Of course, it's better to be at the start of the waterfall than at the end, but everyone usually gets their fill.

Summer somen

Serves: 2
Preparation: 15 minutes
Cooking: about 15 minutes + 20 minutes standing

10 dried shiitake mushrooms
2 tbsp sake
2 tbsp sugar
2 tbsp light soy sauce
270g packet dried somen noodles
1 sheet nori
1 tbsp thinly sliced spring onion (green part only)
1 tsp grated ginger
250 ml mentsuyu (Pantry, page 26)

1. Place the shiitake mushrooms in a heatproof bowl with 500ml boiling water. Leave for 20 minutes to rehydrate and then drain, keeping the liquid.

2. Discard the stalks from the shiitake and thinly slice the caps. Combine the shiitake, sake, sugar, soy sauce and 5 tablespoons of the soaking liquid in a small saucepan. Cover the contents with a cartouche and simmer for 10 minutes. Transfer to a small bowl. (At this point you can chill or serve at room temperature.)

3. Cook the noodles according to packet instructions. Drain, then transfer to a large bowl of iced water.

4. Toast the nori by holding it with tongs over a naked flame. Slice or crumble into small pieces. Place the spring onion and ginger on a small plate (these are the 'yakumi' for the dish and add a piquant element to each mouthful).

5. To serve, put the mentsuyu in a small bowl and serve with the nori, mushrooms and yakumi condiments. To eat the dish put a little each of the mushrooms, nori and yakumi into the mentsuyu to make a dipping sauce. Take the noodles directly out of the water, dunk them into the dipping sauce, then pop straight into your mouth.

Note: *A cartouche is a round of baking paper, cut to fit neatly and sit on the surface of the food as it cooks, to keep in moisture.*

Gong bao chicken (also known as kung pao chicken under the old system of romanisation) is a Sichuanese dish of fried chicken breast. It catches the eye immediately due to the sheer number of red chillies in the dish. It's your choice how many of the chillies you want to eat and, if you avoid them, the dish can be comparatively mild. Dried large red chillies are best for this dish, but if you can't find them just use dried small chillies.

Gong bao chicken

Serves: 2
Preparation: 25 minutes
Cooking: about 15 minutes

80g peanuts
2 chicken breasts, cut into 1.5cm cubes
1 quantity basic stir-fry marinade (On stir-frying, page 37)
12 large dried red chillies, or 15–20 small ones
2 tbsp neutral-flavoured oil
2 tsp Sichuan peppercorns
2 garlic cloves, crushed
1 tsp grated ginger
1 bunch spring onions, white part only, cut into 1.5cm lengths

Sauce
1 tbsp caster sugar
1 tbsp Chianking black vinegar
1 tsp sesame oil
1 tsp dark soy sauce
1 tsp light soy sauce
60ml everyday soup stock (Pantry, page 14), chicken stock or water
1 tsp cornflour

1. Preheat the oven to 180°C. Place the peanuts on a baking tray and roast for a few minutes until golden. Set aside. Toss the chicken in the stir-fry marinade and set aside in the fridge.

2. To make the sauce, mix together all the ingredients to form a slurry.

3. Remove the stalks from the chillies and shake out the seeds. If using large chillies, cut them into large chunks; if using small chillies, keep them whole. Heat the oil in a wok over medium heat and add the chillies and peppercorns. Stir-fry for just a few seconds until the peppercorns pop and the chillies crisp in the oil.

4. Add the chicken to the wok, keeping it moving so that it doesn't colour too much, and cook until the chicken is opaque on the surface. Add the garlic, ginger and spring onions and stir-fry for 1–2 minutes until the chicken is nearly cooked (take care not to overcook the chicken breast or it will be dry). Add the sauce and toss for 1 minute or so until thickened and glossy. Stir in the peanuts and serve.

In Malay nasi lemak means 'coconut rice', and the rice is really what this dish is all about. It is a classic hawker dish that makes a near-perfect breakfast or lunch. I love the combination of sweet sambal, fragrant rice and salty duck eggs. When ordered from a street stall, this dish can be served with any number of accompaniments from curries and sambals to fried chicken. I think it's best served on a banana leaf and eaten with your hands.

Nasi lemak

Serves: 6
Preparation: 15 minutes
Cooking: 30 minutes

450g jasmine rice
180ml coconut cream
½ tsp salt
3 pandan leaves, tied together into a knot
6 salted duck eggs
40g dried anchovies (ikan bilis)
vegetable oil, to deep-fry
40g peanuts
1 pinch caster sugar
¼ tsp sea salt flakes
½ continental cucumber, peeled and thinly sliced
sambal assam (Pantry, page 23), sambal prawns, beef rendang or curry kapitan, to serve

1. Put the rice into a sieve and wash under running water until the water runs clear. Put in a large saucepan with the coconut cream, salt and pandan. Add enough water to come about 2cm over the top of the rice. Simmer over medium heat until the water forms steam holes in the top of the rice. Reduce the heat to very low and cover with a tight-fitting lid. Steam for about 15 minutes. Remove from the heat and leave to steam for a further 5 minutes. Remove the lid and turn the rice with a rice paddle for 30 seconds or so to drive off the steam. Put the lid back on until ready to serve.

2. Meanwhile, boil the duck eggs for 8½ minutes at a rolling boil and then plunge into iced water to stop the cooking process. Peel and cut in half.

3. Meanwhile, rinse the anchovies briefly in cold water and pat dry on paper towel. Half-fill a small saucepan with oil and heat to 160°C. Deep-fry the anchovies and peanuts for 2 minutes until golden brown. Drain on paper towel. Toss the anchovies and peanuts with the sugar and salt.

4. Serve the rice in a mound (use a small rice bowl to make a neat serving) on a plate or a banana leaf with the cucumber, eggs, anchovy and peanut mixture and any accompaniments.

Note: *I like to keep the anchovies separate from the sambal assam when I serve, just to keep them crunchier. If you prefer, you can stir them through the sambal assam.*

Okonomiyaki ('the things you like, fried') is one of my favourite Japanese foods and incredibly easy to make. When I was living in Japan, I spent many nights in my local restaurant chatting to the owner over a beer and a few slices of okonomiyaki. This version contains prawns and cheese, but feel free to experiment with whatever you have to hand.

Prawn and cheese okonomiyaki

Makes: 2 large okonomiyaki, to serve 2–3
Preparation: 20 minutes
Cooking: 25 minutes

300g shredded cabbage
25g tenkasu (see On tempura, page 41)
20g benishouga (red pickled ginger, see Note)
100g raw peeled prawns, cut into 1cm pieces
2 tbsp neutral-flavoured oil
60g grated cheddar cheese
125ml Otafuku okonomiyaki sauce
Kewpie mayonnaise, 2 tbsp aonori (powdered green laver) and dried bonito flakes, to serve

Okonomiyaki batter
220g plain flour
60g potato flour or cornflour
200ml ichiban dashi (Pantry, page 15)
2 eggs

1. To make the batter, whisk the ingredients into a smooth thick paste. It is better to make the okonomiyaki separately, so divide the batter equally between two bowls.

2. Divide the cabbage, tenkasu and benishouga equally between the bowls and stir well. Add half the prawns to each bowl and mix well.

3. Heat a large frying pan over medium heat and add half the oil. Take one of the bowls and add half the mixture to the pan. Spread out to a 15cm circle, scatter with half the cheese and then pour the other half of the mixture on top. Cook for 7 minutes until the base is well browned. Flip over and poke a few large holes in the top to let steam escape. Cook for 5 minutes until cooked through.

4. Transfer to a serving plate and brush with half the Otafuku sauce. Squeeze mayonnaise over the top in a criss-cross pattern and scatter with aonori and bonito flakes. Serve with extra mayonnaise on the side. Make the other okonomiyaki in the same way.

Note: *Benishouga is not the same as the pink gari used for sushi; it is much more red, but pink ginger can be used as a substitute. If you can't find Otafuku sauce at your local Asian supermarket, use Bulldog tonkatsu sauce, or make a reasonable substitute with 5 tbsp tomato sauce mixed with 1 tbsp each of dark soy sauce and Worcestershire sauce and ¼ teaspoon of mustard powder.*

Classic Vietnamese phở is a beautiful, fragrant noodle soup. The heat from the broth lightly cooks thin slices of raw beef, while sulphur compounds in the grilled onion combine with star anise to give the broth a meaty umami flavour that works well with mountains of fresh herbs. I often make phở after buying roasted Chinese-style duck — the leftover carcass can be added to the beef bones for the stock.

Phở

Serves: 1 (also makes about 4 litres broth, see Note)
Preparation: 30 minutes
Cooking: about 3½ hours

Phở broth
2.5kg beef knuckle and leg marrow bones
2 brown onions, unpeeled
10cm piece ginger, unpeeled
40g yellow rock sugar
2 black cardamom pods
6 star anise
2 cinnamon quills
2 tsp each fennel seeds, coriander seeds and cloves
60ml fish sauce

Bowl stuff (per serve)
¼ small brown onion
50g rump steak, tri-tip or flank
1 handful thin dried rice stick noodles
1 spring onion, finely sliced

Plate stuff (per serve)
bean sprouts
fresh coriander, mint, Vietnamese mint and
    Thai basil
red birds-eye chillies, sliced
lemon wedges

Sriracha chilli sauce and hoisin sauce, to serve

1. For the broth, put the beef bones in a large stockpot and cover with cold water. Bring the water to the boil and cook for 5 minutes. Pour off the water, rinse the blanched bones in cold water and put back into the stockpot. Cover again with cold water.

2. Char the onions and ginger on a barbecue or in a grill pan over a high flame. Peel off the blackened skins of the onion and ginger and add the roasted flesh to the pot with the bones. Add the rest of the broth ingredients and heat gently until the broth is just simmering. Cover the pan and simmer for 3½ hours, skimming the surface regularly to remove any fat and scum. Strain the broth and discard the bones and aromatics. Return the broth to the pot and bring to the boil.

3. For the bowl stuff, slice the onion as thinly as possible and soak in cold water for 20 minutes to remove the sharpness. Chill the steak in the freezer for 20 minutes, slice as thinly as possible, then return to room temperature. Blanch the noodles in boiling water for 20–30 seconds until just softened.

4. Place the noodles into a bowl and cover with the raw beef, onion and spring onion. Pour on the boiling broth so that it cooks the thinly sliced beef. Serve immediately with the plate stuff to be added as you eat and separate dipping bowls of Sriracha chilli sauce and hoisin sauce. Some people like to add the sauces to the bowl of soup but I think this overpowers the taste of the broth. I keep them on the side to dip the beef into.

Note: *The recipe makes quite a lot of broth, which can be kept for up to a month in the freezer.*

There are many different kinds of laksa in Malaysia. The Penang laksa that I grew up with is a fishy broth soured with tamarind that would be quite alien to the average Western laksa-eater. What we in Australia call 'laksa' is known in Malaysia as laksa lemak ('coconut laksa'). This is the more common dish across South-East Asia, with near-identical versions found in Singaporean and Thai kitchens.

Laksa lemak

Serves: 4
Preparation: 15 minutes
Cooking: 20 minutes

80g dried vermicelli rice noodles
450g thin fresh hokkien noodles
1 litre chicken, fish or everyday soup stock (Pantry, page 14)
1 tbsp fish sauce
1 tsp salt
4 fried fishcakes, thinly sliced
2 chicken thigh fillets
125g bean sprouts
1 tbsp neutral-flavoured oil
¼ quantity curry laksa paste (Pantry, page 22)
400ml coconut cream
12 prawns, peeled and deveined, tails intact
200g squid, cleaned, scored and cut into triangles
8 fried tofu puffs, quartered
Vietnamese mint leaves and fried shallots, to serve

1. Put the dried noodles in a heatproof bowl and cover with boiling water. Leave to soak for 10 minutes and then drain. Put the hokkien noodles in a heatproof bowl, cover with boiling water and separate with a chopstick or tongs. Leave to soak for 2 minutes and then drain.

2. Meanwhile, put the stock, fish sauce and salt in a small saucepan and bring to a low boil. Add the fishcake and cook for 2 minutes, then lift out and set aside. Add the chicken to the stock and poach for 5 minutes, then lift out, cool and shred. Blanch the bean sprouts for 30 seconds in the stock, then lift out and drain. Keep the poaching stock.

3. Heat the oil in a wok or large saucepan over low heat and add the curry laksa paste. Fry for 5 minutes until fragrant and the oil separates from the paste. Add the poaching stock and bring to the boil. Reduce the heat and simmer for 2 minutes, then add coconut cream and cook for a further 2 minutes.

4. Add the prawns, squid and tofu to the wok and simmer for 3 minutes until the squid and prawns are cooked through. Adjust the seasoning with fish sauce, sugar or lime juice if necessary.

5. Put the noodles in serving bowls and top with the chicken and fishcake. Add the hot laksa soup and top with the blanched bean sprouts. Scatter with Vietnamese mint and fried shallots.

This lovely sweet is often known in English as 'honeycomb cake', but its Malay name is kuih sarang semut, which actually translates as 'ants' nest cake'. The cracks and tracks through the cake not only give it its name, but also a deliciously soft, moist texture with a hint of bitterness from the dark caramel. This is my Uncle Choon's never-fail recipe.

Ants' nest cake

Serves: 8–10
Preparation: 30 minutes
Cooking: 50 minutes + 20 minutes cooling

220g caster sugar
85g unsalted butter, softened
½ tsp vanilla extract
4 eggs, at room temperature
125ml condensed milk
150g plain flour
½ tsp bicarbonate of soda

1. Put the sugar into a medium saucepan and heat gently, swirling the pan occasionally, until melted to a dark caramel. Reduce the heat to low and add 250ml water (it will spit, so stand back). The caramel will solidify but continue to stir over low heat until no lumps remain and you have a thin liquid caramel. Set aside to cool to room temperature, stirring occasionally.

2. Preheat the oven to 170°C. Grease an 18cm round cake tin and line the base with baking paper. Cream the butter and vanilla extract in a large bowl until the butter becomes slightly pale.

3. In a separate bowl, whisk the eggs until well combined. Add the eggs, condensed milk and caramel to the creamed butter and whisk to combine. Sift together the flour and bicarbonate of soda and use the whisk to gently stir into the butter mixture. Don't worry that the butter doesn't mix in evenly — this is how it should be.

4. Pour the cake batter into the tin and leave for a minute or two. Bake for 50 minutes or until the cake is springy to a gentle touch in the centre. Leave to cool in the tin, then run a knife around the edge before turning out. This is excellent with Malaysian coffee (or any coffee, really).

*This Chinese restaurant staple is often made in
a very simple way with artificially coloured and
flavoured mango jelly crystals and evaporated milk.
This natural version is delicious and creamy and
uses beautiful fresh Australian mangoes.*

Mango pudding

Serves: 6
Preparation: 20 minutes
Cooking: 3 hours setting

4–5 ripe mangoes
3 sheets titanium-strength gelatine
375ml evaporated milk
90g caster sugar

1. Peel the mangoes, roughly chop and purée in a
   blender or food processor. Pass through a sieve
   and measure out 500ml fresh mango purée.

2. Soak the gelatine in a bowl of cold water for about
   3 minutes to soften. Mix 300ml of the evaporated
   milk (keep the rest for serving) with the sugar
   and 170ml water in a small saucepan and bring to
   a simmer.

3. Squeeze any excess water from the gelatine and
   whisk into the milk mixture until completely
   dissolved. Remove from the heat, add the mango
   purée and whisk until well combined.

4. Pour into small glasses and refrigerate for
   about 3 hours until set. Serve drizzled with
   evaporated milk.

This is generally known as 'sago pudding'. The 'pearls' used for this recipe are dried starch balls extracted from sago or tapioca starch. Their flavours are almost identical although tapioca pearls are more widely available than true sago. Use either.

Pearl pudding

Serves: 8
Preparation: 30 minutes
Cooking: 50 minutes + 2 hours setting

250g dried sago or tapioca pearls

Palm sugar syrup
200g palm sugar, grated or chopped
40g dark brown sugar
3 pandan leaves, roughly chopped
20g ginger, sliced

Salted coconut cream
400ml thick coconut cream
¼ tsp fine salt

1. Lightly oil eight 125ml dariole moulds. Bring 1.25 litres water to the boil in a large pot and add the sago. Cook over medium-low heat, stirring regularly with a wooden spoon to prevent the sago catching on the bottom, for about 30 minutes until tender and clear.

2. Pour or ladle half the sago into a sieve and rinse under cold running water. Use a spatula to stir the sago and let the water run through it. Drain and transfer to a bowl. Repeat with the rest of the sago. Spoon equally into the dariole moulds and refrigerate for 2 hours until set.

3. To make the palm sugar syrup, place all the ingredients into a small saucepan, add 300ml water and stir to dissolve the sugar. Bring to the boil, reduce the heat slightly and simmer for about 15 minutes until thickened and reduced to about 250ml. Strain and set aside.

4. To make the salted coconut cream, stir together the coconut cream and salt in a bowl until the salt has dissolved. (It's best not to heat this to preserve the raw flavour of the coconut cream.)

5. Turn out the puddings onto plates and serve with the salted coconut cream and palm sugar syrup.

This simple Okinawan fried doughnut is a combination of Japanese and Chinese techniques common to Okinawan cuisine. Throughout history the kingdom of Ryukyu (now Okinawa) has had close political, cultural and military ties with both nations and those relationships have also left an indelible imprint on the kitchens of the region.

Sataa andagi

Makes: about 40
Preparation: 10 minutes
Cooking: 12 minutes

2 eggs
125ml pouring cream
¼ tsp vanilla paste
300g plain flour
2 tsp baking powder
220g caster sugar
¼ tsp salt
vegetable oil, to deep-fry

1. Whisk the eggs, cream and vanilla together in a large bowl. Sift together the flour, baking powder, sugar and salt. Fold into the egg mixture until well combined.

2. Half-fill a large saucepan with oil and heat to 180°C. Drop teaspoonfuls of dough into the hot oil, cooking about 6 at a time. Fry for 2 minutes until golden brown and risen to the surface. Lift out with a slotted spoon and drain on paper towels. They will become crisp on cooling.

Note: *Use one teaspoon to scoop spoonfuls of dough and another spoon to scrape the dough into the oil. Don't make the andagi too large or they won't be cooked in the centre. Test a couple to make sure you have it right.*

This vividly coloured cake is one of the most memorable images of my childhood. Its nine layers are considered lucky. This is my grandmother's recipe and I have used traditional colours here, but some like to add other food colourings to make dramatically tinted layers.

Nine layer cake (kuih lapis)

Makes: about 16 pieces
Preparation: 20 minutes
Cooking: 45 minutes + 1 hour standing

180g rice flour
15g tapioca flour (or cornflour)
180g caster sugar
3 pandan leaves, tied together in a knot
200ml coconut cream
1 large pinch sea salt flakes
orange food colouring (or red and yellow mixed)
pink or red food colouring
vegetable oil, to brush

1. Combine the flours in a bowl and mix in 150ml water. Leave to stand for 1 hour. Meanwhile, combine the sugar, pandan leaves and 350ml water in a saucepan and stir over medium-low heat until the sugar has completely dissolved. Leave to cool to room temperature and then remove the pandan leaves.

2. Beat the coconut cream and salt into the sugar syrup and then add to the flour mixture. Whisk together well and then pass the batter through a fine sieve to remove any lumps.

3. Measure 150ml of the batter and place in a small bowl. Divide the remaining batter equally between 2 bowls. Add orange food colouring to the small bowl to tint the batter deep orange. Add pink or red colouring to another bowl to give candy pink batter. The third bowl should remain white.

4. Heat a shallow 18cm square cake tin in a bamboo steamer for 5 minutes. Brush the inside of the tin with a very small amount of oil and pour in 80ml of the white mixture. Steam over low-medium heat for 3 minutes until just set but still sticky when touched. Wash the measuring cup and measure 80ml of the pink mixture. Pour this directly on top of the white mixture. Steam for a further 3 minutes. It is very important to use accurate measurements so that the layers of the cake are an even thickness.

5. Repeat until you have 8 alternating layers: 4 white and 4 pink, steaming each layer for 3 minutes as it is added. For the final 9th layer, pour on the orange mixture. Wrap the lid of the steamer in a clean tea towel before covering — this will absorb excess steam and prevent condensation dripping onto the cake. Steam for about 10 minutes until the top has set and does not stick to your fingers when touched. Leave to cool completely in the tin, then cut into diamond shapes with a knife or serrated cutter.

Too often, we pigeonhole ourselves as cooks, telling ourselves we 'can't bake' or 'can't cook Chinese food'. We resign ourselves and our kitchens to the same safe procession of daily dishes. The essence of The New Kitchen is the boldness and fearlessness of those culinary pioneers who are not afraid to venture into the unknown.

When I was growing up there was little or no emphasis on the creation of new dishes or flavours. All but the most high-end restaurants served a menu of safe classics, perhaps with that eating house's trademark minor variation. Families at home cooked in the same way and, although there were differences between my grandmother's bolognese and your grandmother's bolognese, they were both bolognese.

Fortunately, food in Australia today is going through a bold period of innovation and we are more open to expanding our culinary horizons. The recipes of The New Kitchen are inspired by the flavours and techniques of Asia, but they are undeniably Australian creations.

TheNewKitchen

This dish combines two of my favourite foods in the world: laksa and fried chicken. On family road trips around Malaysia we would sample as many plates of fried chicken from roadside stalls as our stomachs would allow. I can't say if we ever found the perfect fried chicken — it was really more about the journey than the destination.

Laksa fried chicken

Serves: 4–6
Preparation: 35 minutes + overnight marinating
Cooking: 25 minutes

1 whole chicken, jointed into 10 pieces
1 cup curry laksa paste (Pantry, page 22)
125ml coconut cream
neutral-flavoured oil, to deep-fry
75g cornflour
75g plain flour
90g desiccated coconut

Laksa leaf sauce
1 tbsp shredded laksa leaf (Vietnamese mint)
80ml rice wine vinegar
1 tbsp caster sugar
2 tbsp light soy sauce
1 tbsp fish sauce
1 garlic clove, finely chopped
3 red birds-eye chillies, seeded and finely chopped

1. Score deep cuts about 3 cm apart in any large pieces of chicken to allow the marinade to penetrate. Mix together the laksa paste and coconut cream and use to coat the chicken. Leave in the fridge overnight, removing 1 hour before cooking to return to room temperature.

2. Half-fill a large saucepan with oil and heat to 160°C. Mix together the flours and coconut. Remove the chicken from the marinade, leaving much of the liquid still clinging to it, and coat in the flour and coconut mixture. Deep-fry in batches until golden brown and cooked through (about 10–12 minutes for thigh pieces, 7–8 minutes for breast pieces and 4–5 minutes for wings). Drain on paper towel.

3. To make the laksa leaf sauce, mix together all the ingredients in a bowl and stir until the sugar has dissolved. Serve with the chicken.

There is a nice balance to this dish that makes it great comfort food. The caramelised pork is coated in pieces of sticky-but-crisp garlic that balance the soft texture of the rice. In turn, the acidity of the pickles and bitterness of the lemon paste cut through the sweet oiliness of the pork.

Black belly rice bowl (with lemon paste and pickled chilli)

Serves: 2
Preparation: 15 minutes
Cooking: 1 hour 15 minutes

500g pork belly
750ml everyday soup stock (Pantry, page 14) or water
1 tbsp neutral-flavoured oil
3 garlic cloves, chopped
2 tsp dark soy sauce
1 tsp caster sugar
¼ tsp sea salt flakes
1 tbsp Cheong Chan cooking caramel
3 cups cooked Japanese short-grain rice
ninety-second greens (overleaf)
1 tbsp lemon paste (Pantry, page 19)
1 tbsp pickled chillies (Pantry, page 23)

1. Place the pork belly in a large saucepan and cover with cold water. Bring to the boil then drain off the water. Cover the pork again with the stock or water. Bring to the boil, reduce the heat to medium-low and simmer, partially covered, for 1 hour. Leave to rest for 10 minutes and then chop the pork into bite-sized pieces. (This can be done a day in advance, but the pork should be chilled in the fridge if you are not frying it straight away.)

2. Heat the oil in a wok over high heat and stir-fry the garlic until it just starts to colour. Add the pork and stir-fry for 5 minutes until the pork and garlic are browned. Add the soy, sugar, salt and cooking caramel and stir-fry for 1–2 minutes until the sugar forms a sticky caramel.

3. Divide the rice between 2 rice bowls and top with the ninety-second greens and then the sticky pork (use a slotted spoon to drain some of the oil from the pork). Daub lemon paste over the pork and scatter with pickled chillies.

This is the fastest, easiest and tastiest way to cook greens that I know. When it's this easy to add delicious greenery to your meal there is really no excuse for exclusive carnivorousness.

Ninety-second greens

Serves: 4 as a side dish
Preparation and cooking: 90 seconds

1 bunch Chinese or English spinach (see Note)
1 tbsp salt
2 tsp neutral-flavoured oil

Bring 500ml water to the boil. Once the water boils your time starts...

0–30 seconds: Open the fridge, pull out the Chinese spinach and chop off the root end. Wash the greens thoroughly, either under the tap or in a sink of water. Shake off the excess water and cut into 7cm lengths.

30–60 seconds: Add half the salt to the boiling water, stir and drop in the greens (stalks first, leaves last). Add the oil and remaining salt on top of the greens and, using chopsticks or tongs, agitate the greens to 'wash off' the oil and salt in the boiling water. Enough of the salt and oil will stick to the leaves to flavour them and the remaining salt will dissolve in the water. Cook for about 30 seconds until tender.

60–90 seconds: Pull the greens out with tongs or chopsticks and place in a colander. Use the tongs or chopsticks to squeeze out the excess moisture and lift into your bowl, ready to eat.

Note: *You can use other Asian greens here but it will affect cooking times.*

My grandmother always prepares our Christmas turkey with the most amazing glutinous rice stuffing. Here I've used that stuffing in a boned pork trotter. The boning process is not simple, but persevere and you will have a delicious little morsel of pork trotter to enjoy. I serve this with the same chilli sauce that I make for Hainanese chicken rice (page 49).

Glutinous rice-stuffed pork trotter

Serves: 4
Preparation: 45 minutes + overnight soaking
Cooking: 3 hours 45 minutes

4 pig's trotters
1.5 litres aromatic master stock (Pantry, page 18)
5 dried shiitake mushrooms
250g white glutinous rice, washed and soaked
   overnight in plenty of water
2 lap cheong (Chinese pork sausages)
1 tsp light soy sauce
1 tsp dark soy sauce
¼ tsp sea salt flakes
¼ tsp ground white pepper
1 tsp caster sugar
1 tsp sesame oil
4 sheets caul fat (ask your butcher)
2 tbsp pork lard, or neutral-flavoured oil
chilli sauce, to serve

1. Use a disposable razor (without lubricating strip) to shave any hairs off the trotters or burn them off with a blowtorch. Bone the pork trotters by cutting around the bone from the leg end and peeling back the skin towards the end of the foot, while continuing to cut around the bone. Roll the skin down towards the nails of the rearmost toes and cut at the join so that the nails remain with the skin. Crack the bone at the joint at the base of the hoof and remove the bone. Invert the bone and reinsert into the trotter and secure the meat around the loose bone with string.

2. Place the trotters in a large saucepan and cover with master stock. Bring to a simmer, cover the pan and cook for 2½ hours until the trotters are very tender. Remove from the liquid, untie the string and remove the bone.

3. Meanwhile, rinse the shiitake mushrooms briefly, place in a heatproof bowl and cover with boiling water. Soak for 30 minutes. Discard the stalks and thinly slice the caps.

4. Meanwhile, place a layer of muslin over the base of a large bamboo steamer. Drain the rice and spread over the muslin. Steam for 30 minutes. Remove the rice and cool. Steam the lap cheong for 10 minutes then thinly slice.

5. Combine the mushrooms, lap cheong, rice, soy sauces, salt, pepper, sugar and sesame oil in a large bowl. Stuff into the trotters and wrap the entire trotter in caul fat. Steam in a bamboo steamer for 30 minutes.

6. Heat the pork lard in a frying pan and fry the trotters until crisping. Slice and serve with a little chilli sauce.

Dan dan mian is a popular Sichuanese noodle dish of minced pork in a spicy sauce, often with sesame paste. Here I've taken the flavours of dan dan mian and combined them with minced beef over rice. The green peas give a burst of freshness and sweetness. I've layered the peas and spring onions through the dish as a bit of a surprise, but also to make it easier to eat — with a spoon in front of the TV!

Spicy minced beef dan dan rice bowl

Serves: 2
Preparation: 15 minutes
Cooking: 10 minutes

3 tbsp sesame seeds
1½ tsp rice wine vinegar
1½ tsp caster sugar
1 tbsp light soy sauce
2 tbsp neutral-flavoured oil
½ tsp Sichuan peppercorns
1 tbsp Tianjin preserved vegetable (see Note)
1 tbsp chilli and garlic oil (Pantry, page 19)
250g minced beef
3 cups cooked Japanese short-grain rice
150g peas, cooked
4 spring onions (green part only), sliced

1. Toast the sesame seeds in a dry frying pan over medium heat for about 2 minutes until fragrant. Put in a mortar with the vinegar, sugar and light soy sauce and grind to a paste. Remove from the mortar and set aside (always remove from the mortar, rather than trying to add something to a hot wok from a heavy stone bowl).

2. Heat the oil in a wok and stir-fry the Sichuan peppercorns for a few seconds until fragrant and starting to colour. Add the Tianjin preserved vegetable and fry for 30 seconds. Add the chilli and garlic oil and fry for a few more seconds, then add the beef and stir-fry, breaking up any lumps, for 3–4 minutes until well browned. Add the sesame paste and toss together. Season with salt.

3. Place a few spoonfuls of rice in each rice bowl. Add the peas, keeping a few to top the bowl. Add another layer of rice and cover with spring onion, again keeping a few to top the bowl. The heat from the rice will soften the onion. Cover with the remaining rice and then spoon the beef mixture over the top. Garnish with peas and spring onion as a hint of what is hidden under the rice.

Note: *Tianjin preserved vegetable is Chinese shredded pickled cabbage, available in jars from Asian food shops.*

This is a great healthy dinner that takes only a few minutes to cook from start to finish. It tastes fantastic but is almost totally guilt free.

Aromatic poached fish with chilli and greens

Serves: 2
Preparation: 10 minutes
Cooking: 4–8 minutes

1 litre aromatic master stock (Pantry, page 18)
2 skinless fillets (180g each) firm white fish, such as
    ling or monkfish
ninety-second greens (page 143), to serve
cooked rice and 2 tsp chilli and garlic oil
    (Pantry, page 19), to serve

1. Bring the master stock to a simmer in a medium saucepan. Gently add the fish fillets so that they are completely covered with stock. Keep the stock at just below a simmer.

2. Poach the fish for 4–8 minutes, depending on the thickness of the fillets, until just opaque and with easily flaking flesh.

3. Remove the fish from the stock and serve on top of the ninety-second greens. Splash a little poaching liquid over the fish and top with a spoonful of chilli and garlic oil. Serve with rice.

This dish is a Thai–Japanese mix that may sound strange but makes perfect sense to me! The miso works with the salty-savoury flavours of the curry paste and the sweetness of the coconut cream to add an interesting complexity. Both miso and green curry are great matches for seafood and eggplant, so be warned: once you've tried this you may never go back to making simple Thai green curries. If you don't want to make your own green curry paste, use a good-quality bought variety.

White miso green curry with seafood

Serves: 4
Preparation: 30 minutes
Cooking: 30 minutes

3 tbsp shredded bamboo shoots, drained (optional)
1 eggplant (about 250g)
400ml coconut cream
375ml ichiban dashi (Pantry, page 15)
8 black mussels, cleaned and debearded
12 green prawns, peeled and deveined, tails intact
200g firm white fish fillets, skin removed, cut into
    large chunks
12 scallops
2 tbsp white miso paste
2 tbsp mirin, plus extra for seasoning
1 small handful coriander leaves
1 small handful Thai basil leaves
juice of ½ lime
fish sauce, to taste

Thai green curry paste (see Note)
1½ tsp cumin seeds
1½ tsp coriander seeds
1 tsp white peppercorns
5 coriander roots (keep the leaves)
2 lemongrass stalks (white part only), roughly sliced
5cm piece galangal, peeled
10 garlic cloves, roughly chopped
10 green birds-eye chillies
4 long green chillies
4 eschalots, sliced
5 kaffir lime leaves, spines removed, finely sliced
3 tsp shrimp paste

1. To make the curry paste, roast the cumin and coriander seeds in a dry frying pan over low heat for 2–3 minutes until fragrant. Cool, then grind to a powder with the peppercorns, using a mortar and pestle or spice grinder. If you have a large enough mortar, continue building the paste with your mortar and pestle. If not, transfer to a food processor. Add the remaining curry paste ingredients a little at a time and pound or process until fairly smooth. (If you like a mild curry paste, adjust the proportion of chillies but don't leave out too many or the colour will suffer. Also, using miso in this dish produces a milder green curry than usual.)

2. Bring 500ml water to the boil in a small saucepan. Add the bamboo and simmer for 15 minutes. Rinse in cold water and drain well. Cut the eggplant into 2cm cubes and place in a colander. Salt the eggplant liberally and leave to drain while you cook the curry sauce.

3. Bring the coconut cream to the boil in a large wok or saucepan and add 4 tbsp of the curry paste (freeze the remainder). Cook over low heat, stirring occasionally, for about 15 minutes until the oil separates from the coconut cream and forms an oily sheen on the surface of the sauce. Add the dashi and return to a simmer.

4. Rinse the eggplant and add to the curry sauce. Cook for 7 minutes over medium heat until the eggplant is becoming tender. Add the bamboo and seafood and cook for 4 minutes until the mussels open and the fish and prawns are cooked through. Remove from the heat.

5. Dissolve the miso and mirin in about 125ml boiling water. Stir into the curry. Stir in the coriander leaves, basil and lime juice. Taste the curry and adjust the seasoning with more fish sauce (salt), lime juice (acidity) or mirin (sweetness) if needed. Miso is quite salty so additional fish sauce may not be required.

Note: *This makes enough curry paste (8 tablespoons) for 2 batches of curry. Keep the remaining paste in an airtight container in the freezer for next time.*

My version of the traditional Thai snack miang kham uses a tiny Scotch quail egg with prawn mince on top of a sticky coconut sambal. Betel leaves are delicious and are used here as edible serving plates: they have become extremely popular in Australia in recent years and so are relatively easy to find in Asian grocery stores.

Scotch quail egg 'miang kham'

Makes: 12
Preparation: 30 minutes + 1 hour chilling
Cooking: 20 minutes

6 quail eggs
1 large eschalot, sliced
2 garlic cloves, sliced
1 tsp grated ginger
12 large raw prawns, peeled, deveined and cut into large chunks
1 tbsp fish sauce
75g plain flour
2 eggs, lightly beaten
40g panko breadcrumbs
vegetable oil, to deep-fry
12 betel leaves, to serve

Coconut and chilli sambal
40g raw peanuts
45g desiccated coconut
2 whole coriander plants (see Note)
2 tsp neutral-flavoured oil
5 eschalots, sliced
2 garlic cloves, minced
1 tsp grated ginger
3 red birds-eye chillies, seeds removed, finely chopped
1 tbsp fish sauce
2 tbsp Cheong Chan cooking caramel, plus extra to serve
2 tbsp grated palm sugar
2 tbsp everyday soup stock (Pantry, page 14) or chicken stock or water

1. Bring a small saucepan of water to the boil and add the quail eggs. (I find a metal sieve with a handle very useful for adding all the eggs at once.) Boil for 2 minutes then immediately plunge into iced water. Cool, then peel the eggs and set aside.

2. Using a mortar and pestle, grind the eschalot, garlic and ginger to a paste. Add the prawns a few pieces at a time and pound to a smooth paste. Moisten the end of the pestle with fish sauce every so often to season the prawns. Pound until all the fish sauce has been combined and a thick paste has formed. Lift the paste out of the mortar and throw it back down into the bowl a few times with force until it becomes lighter in your hand.

3. Divide the paste into 6 equal portions. With wet hands, cover each egg with prawn paste, then chill in the fridge for 30 minutes or until firm. Roll the chilled eggs in flour, then in beaten egg and finally in panko breadcrumbs. Chill again in the fridge.

4. Half-fill a medium saucepan with oil and heat to 180°C. Deep-fry the eggs in 2 batches for 5 minutes each until browned and cooked through. Drain on paper towels.

5. To make the coconut and chilli sambal, preheat the oven to 200°C. Roast the peanuts on an oven tray for 3–4 minutes until golden and then crush with a mortar and pestle. Roast the coconut in a dry wok, stirring often, until just browned. Transfer to a plate and set aside. Finely slice the coriander roots and chop the stalks and leaves.

6. Heat the oil and fry the eschalots, garlic, ginger and coriander root over medium heat until just starting to brown. Add the chillies, fish sauce, caramel sauce, palm sugar and stock and simmer for 2 minutes. Add the coconut and cook for 2 minutes until the coconut softens. Stir in half the peanuts and most of the coriander leaves and stalks. Set aside to cool.

7. To assemble the dish, lay out the betel leaves and top each with a teaspoon of the sambal. Halve the Scotch eggs and place half on top of each leaf. Top with a little of the reserved peanuts and coriander and drizzle with a little more caramel sauce.

Note: *Use 2 coriander plants (stems, leaves and roots attached), not 2 bunches of coriander.*

Japanese food can be playful and one interestingly named dish is Oyakodon. 'Oyako' means 'parent and child' and 'don' is a contraction of 'donburi' — 'rice bowl'. Oyakodon is a delicious combination of chicken and just-set eggs served over rice. Here I've taken the parent and child concept and applied it to a duck rice bowl, with a nod to the flavours of canard a l'orange. The rich saltiness of duck and egg is offset by the cleansing acidity of pickled daikon. Buy salted duck eggs that have not been pre-cooked and vacuum-packed — these are often overcooked.

Parent and child duck rice bowl

Serves: 2
Preparation: 10 minutes
Cooking: 15 minutes + 10 minutes standing

2 salted duck eggs
2 duck breast fillets
2 tsp neutral-flavoured oil
2 tbsp finely chopped brown onion
3 tbsp aromatic master stock (Pantry, page 18)
3 cups cooked Japanese short-grain rice
2 tbsp white pickled daikon (Pantry, page 15)
2 tsp finely sliced spring onion (green part only)
1 tsp finely grated orange zest

1. Bring water to the boil in a small saucepan and add the duck eggs. Boil for 8½ minutes and then plunge the eggs into iced water to cool. Peel and set aside.

2. Score the duck skin in a diamond pattern (cut through the fat but not into the meat). Salt the scored side lightly and leave for 10 minutes. Heat the oil in a frying pan over medium heat and cook the duck skin-side-down for 2½ minutes to render out as much fat as possible. Turn and cook the meat side for 1½ minutes. Lift out the duck and leave to rest for at least 2 minutes. Keep the rendered duck fat.

3. Cut the duck into 2cm cubes (it will still be quite rare in the middle, but is going to be cooked again later).

4. Return 2 tsp of the rendered duck fat to the pan and fry the onion over medium heat for 2 minutes until softened. Return the duck to the pan and add the master stock. Toss to coat and cook for about 2 minutes to thicken the sauce and cook the duck through.

5. Spoon the rice into bowls, add the duck, halved duck eggs, white pickled daikon and spring onion. Place the orange zest in a small mound on top of the duck.

There's nothing wrong with serving a great steak as part of a shared meal – just slice it and bring to the table for everyone to try. My three favourite things to eat with steak are all green and these condiments all add to the character of a nice piece of wagyu.

Wagyu with three green things

Serves: 4 as part of a shared meal
Preparation: 15 minutes
Cooking: 3–5 minutes + overnight refrigeration

1 large wagyu sirloin steak (about 300g)
olive oil, to fry
fresh wasabi, to serve (see Note)

Chimichurri
1 handful flat-leaf parsley
1 fresh bay leaf, finely shredded
½ onion
3 garlic cloves
1 tbsp dried oregano
1 tsp hot paprika
1 tbsp sea salt flakes
½ tsp freshly ground black pepper
½ tsp chilli flakes
125ml olive oil
3 tbsp red wine vinegar
2 tbsp lemon juice

Yuzu kocho
finely grated zest of 1 yuzu (or zest of 1 lemon mixed
    with 1 tbsp yuzu juice)
5 large green chillies, seeds removed, chopped
1 tbsp sea salt flakes

1. To make the chimichurri, put the parsley, bay leaf, onion, garlic, oregano, paprika, salt, pepper and chilli flakes in a food processor and process to a paste. I like my chimichurri to be quite smooth but, if you prefer it rough, you can cut the ingredients by hand. Add the oil, vinegar and lemon juice and process again to emulsify. Transfer to a non-reactive bowl or glass jar and refrigerate overnight to let the flavours develop.

2. Meanwhile, to make the yuzu kocho, pound all the ingredients with a mortar and pestle to make a smooth paste. Transfer to a small jar and refrigerate overnight to let the flavours develop.

3. Take the steak from the fridge to come to room temperature 1 hour before cooking. Take the yuzu kocho and chimichurri from the fridge as well to let them reach room temperature for serving. Season the steak well with salt. Heat a heavy-based frying pan or grill pan until very hot and brush with a little oil. Fry the steak, turning every 30 seconds or so, until cooked to your liking. Rest the steak for half the time it took to cook.

4. While the steak is resting, grate the wasabi. Slice the steak and serve with the wasabi, yuzu kocho and chimichurri.

Note: *If fresh wasabi is not available, the best substitute is powdered wasabi mixed with grated daikon radish. This more closely matches the flavour and texture of fresh wasabi than prepared pastes or mixing the powder with water.*

The taste and texture of raw baby vegetables is so delicate that they should be eaten with as little preparation as possible. Just simply clean and trim them and serve with this mayonnaise mixture.

Baby vegetable crudités with red miso mayonnaise

Serves: 1
**Preparation: about 15 minutes, depending
  on vegetables**

assorted baby vegetables (see Note)
ice
1 tbsp Kewpie mayonnaise or yuzu mayonnaise
   (Pantry, page 22)
1 tsp red miso

1. Wash and trim the vegetables well and arrange on a bed of ice.

2. Place the mayonnaise and miso in a small bowl and mix so that they are combined but not a smooth homogenous sauce: there should still be swirls of miso through the mayonnaise. Serve with a small spoon.

Note: *Use a selection of baby vegetables in season. Try carrots, cucumbers, cabbage leaves, lettuce, corn (fresh, not canned), golden baby beetroot, cauliflower, red radish, cherry tomatoes or eggplant.*

The aroma of fennel from this roasting pork is something not to be missed, and the flavour works perfectly with black pepper. The 'pork condiment' is a deliciously piquant alternative to apple sauce that balances the strong flavours of the pork belly.

Fennel and black pepper pork belly with pork condiment

Serves: 4–6
Preparation: 20 minutes + overnight marinating
Cooking: 50 minutes + 20 minutes resting

750g pork belly
2½ tbsp fennel seeds
3 garlic cloves
1 tbsp whole black peppercorns
2 tbsp olive oil
1 tbsp sea salt flakes

Pork condiment
2 granny smith apples, peeled, cored and
   roughly chopped
1 tbsp white vinegar
2 tbsp lemon paste (Pantry, page 19)
1 tbsp dijon mustard
2 tsp honey
salt, to taste

1. Using a disposable razor without a lubricating strip, shave any hairs from the pork belly and trim away any undesirable parts. Put the pork in a colander and pour boiling water over the skin to blanch (you will see the skin tighten). Dry the pork well and poke lots of holes in the skin with a very sharp small knife. The more holes you poke, the better your crackling will be (I make hundreds of holes). Turn the pork over and score cuts into the meat side at 2–3cm intervals across the grain, cutting down to the skin but not through it.

2. Toast the fennel seeds in a dry frying pan over medium heat for 2–3 minutes until fragrant. Pound the fennel, garlic and peppercorns together in a mortar to form a smooth paste, then mix in the oil. Rub the paste into the meat side only, getting well into all the score lines. Do not get any paste on the skin. Place the pork on a rack in a baking tray and rub the sea salt into the skin. Put the tray in the fridge and leave the pork to dry overnight, uncovered. Blot the skin dry with paper towel if moisture pools on it.

3. Preheat the oven to 220°C. Drain any liquid that has pooled in the tray. Put the tray in the oven and roast the pork skin-side-down for 20 minutes. Turn over and roast for a further 20 minutes.

4. Switch the oven to grill, open the door a crack to release steam and grill the pork for 3–5 minutes until the skin crackles. Rest for 15–20 minutes.

5. Meanwhile, to make the pork condiment, put the apples, vinegar and 125ml water in a saucepan. Bring to the boil, then reduce the heat to simmer for 6–8 minutes until tender. Drain, then purée with the lemon paste, mustard and honey. Season with salt to taste.

6. Chop the pork into bite-size pieces and serve with the pork condiment.

In-season and simply prepared are the best ways to enjoy asparagus. This is the perfect spring dish when the markets are overflowing with new season asparagus. For something a little more special, add some grilled scallops.

Steamed asparagus with kushiyaki quail eggs and yuzu mayonnaise

Serves: 4 as part of a shared meal
Preparation: 10 minutes
Cooking: 5 minutes

4 quail eggs
1 tbsp plain flour
1 egg, lightly beaten
20g panko breadcrumbs
vegetable oil, to deep-fry
1 bunch asparagus, trimmed
2 tsp extra virgin olive oil
2 tbsp yuzu mayonnaise (Pantry, page 22)

1. Add the quail eggs to a saucepan of boiling water and cook for 1 minute 50 seconds. Lift out with a slotted spoon and place in a bowl of iced water to stop the cooking process. Peel the eggs carefully (they will still have runny yolks and be quite delicate) and chill them in the fridge.

2. Roll the chilled eggs in flour, then in the beaten egg and finally in the panko breadcrumbs. Half-fill a medium saucepan with oil and heat to 180°C. Deep-fry the eggs for 1 minute until the breadcrumbs are golden. Drain on paper towel.

3. Steam the asparagus over boiling water for 2 minutes until tender. Transfer to a plate, drizzle with extra virgin olive oil and season to taste with sea salt and freshly ground black pepper.

4. Serve the asparagus with the fried quail eggs and yuzu mayonnaise.

This pork belly recipe uses an adaptation of a Thai barbecue sauce — I have added rum to enhance the molasses characteristics of the dish. What I love about this is that it is identifiably Thai but doesn't feature any chilli, so it's great for people who don't like their food too hot. Serve with a cold beer.

Rum and lemongrass roast pork belly

Serves: 4–6
Preparation: 25 minutes
Cooking: 1 hour + 2 hours marinating

1kg skinless, boneless pork belly
chopped coriander, to serve

Marinade
150g palm sugar, roughly chopped
200ml fish sauce
200ml dark soy sauce
6 stalks lemongrass, white part only, thinly sliced
100ml dark rum
6 eschalots, sliced thinly
6 garlic cloves, minced
60ml sesame oil
1 tbsp ground white pepper
125ml coconut cream

1. Preheat the oven to 200°C. To make the marinade, combine all the ingredients except the coconut cream in a saucepan or wok. Bring to the boil, reduce the heat and simmer for 15–20 minutes until reduced by half. Allow to cool and then stir in the coconut cream.

2. Score the fat side of the pork belly in a small diamond pattern, without cutting through the meat. This will assist the fat to render out in the short cooking time. Cut the pork belly across the grain into 5cm wide strips, place in a non-reactive dish and cover with the marinade. Refrigerate for 2 hours. Remove the pork and place in a roasting tin, keeping the marinade.

3. Roast the pork belly for 30 minutes until just cooked through. Alternatively, you could grill the pork on a barbecue. Rest the meat for 10 minutes and then cut into bite-sized pieces.

4. Place the marinade in a small saucepan and bring to the boil. Reduce the heat slightly and simmer for at least 3 minutes to kill any bacteria. Continue to simmer until reduced to a sticky sauce. Pour a tablespoon or two of sauce over each piece of meat and scatter with fresh coriander to serve.

These croquettes make a great snack or canapé and keep well in the fridge until ready to deep-fry. The combination of green tea and peas gives this dish a vibrant and inviting green colour.

Green tea and pea croquettes

Makes: 15 croquettes
Preparation: 20 minutes
Cooking: 6–9 minutes + 1 hour 15 minutes chilling

300g frozen peas
20g unsalted butter
2 tbsp plain flour
1 tbsp grated onion
1 tsp green tea powder (matcha)
¼ tsp salt
3 eggs
1 pinch white pepper
2 tbsp plain flour
40g panko breadcrumbs
vegetable oil, to deep-fry
Kewpie mayonnaise, to serve

1. Boil the peas in a little salted water until tender, then drain. Purée in a food processor until smooth, then add the butter, flour, onion, green tea powder, salt, 1 egg and white pepper and process until smooth.

2. Transfer to a metal bowl and place over a pot of boiling water, making sure that the bottom of the bowl is not touching the water. Cook, stirring, for 3 minutes until the purée is heated through and starting to stiffen. Cover the surface of the purée with cling wrap to prevent a skin forming and put in the fridge for about 1 hour until firm.

3. Using wet hands, form level tablespoons of the cold purée into small balls. Lightly beat the remaining eggs in a bowl. Dip the balls into the flour, then the beaten egg and finally the panko breadcrumbs. Arrange in a single layer on a plate and refrigerate for 15 minutes until firm.

4. Half-fill a medium saucepan with vegetable oil and heat to 180°C. Fry the croquettes in 3 batches for 2–3 minutes each until golden brown. Drain on paper towel. Season with sea salt flakes and rest for 5 minutes before serving with mayonnaise.

Yukhoe is a Korean dish of raw beef in a spicy dressing, often served with nashi pear. It is popular in Japan under the Japanised name 'yukke'. This is a more Japanese version of the dish, served with toasted nori seaweed to wrap. I've chosen to use green apple in this dish instead of the more traditional nashi pear.

Raw beef and green apple yukhoe

Serves: 4 as part of a shared meal
Preparation: 15 minutes
Cooking: 4 minutes

1 tsp white sesame seeds
1 tsp pine nuts
120g beef fillet
1 nori sheet, to serve
1 quail egg yolk
20g green apple, unpeeled, sliced

Sauce
1 garlic clove, crushed
½ tsp grated ginger
½ tsp caster sugar
1 tsp kochujang (Korean chilli bean paste)
2 tsp sesame oil
2 tsp light soy sauce
1 tsp rice wine vinegar
¼ tsp chilli powder

1. To make the sauce, pound the garlic and ginger together with a mortar and pestle. Add the sugar and kochujang and pound to a paste. Mix in the sesame oil, soy sauce, rice wine vinegar and chilli powder.

2. Toast the sesame seeds and pine nuts in a dry frying pan over medium heat for about 2 minutes until fragrant. Cut the beef into 5mm medallions, then into 5mm strips. Cut the nori sheet into quarters. Toast the nori by holding it with tongs over a naked flame.

3. Combine the toasted seeds and nuts, sauce and beef in a bowl and toss well. Pile the beef onto a serving plate. Top the beef with the quail egg yolk and serve with the sliced apple and nori sheets.

4. To eat, mix the egg yolk and beef together, then wrap the beef and a little sliced apple in nori and pop it straight into your mouth.

Perhaps strangely, the inspiration for this is the 1953 Coronation Chicken created for Queen Elizabeth. When I read about it at the age of 9, it had never dawned on me that new dishes could be 'created' by chefs. Until then, I had only eaten traditional food cooked by my parents and grandparents. The concept that I could challenge food to develop and grow was a real epiphany for me. This is called Royal chicken because I have a bizarre but unshakable vision of the Queen sitting back with a bowl of this creamy chicken stir-fry in front of EastEnders on the telly.

'Royal chicken' with spinach and garlic rice

Serves: 2
Preparation: 15 minutes
Cooking: about 10 minutes

250g chicken thigh fillets, thinly sliced
1 tbsp basic stir-fry marinade (On stir-frying, page 37)
1 tbsp olive oil
½ brown onion, sliced
50g shimeji mushrooms, broken into clumps, hard ends trimmed
½ tsp sea salt flakes
¼ tsp ground black pepper
1 tbsp mentsuyu (Pantry, page 26)
50ml pouring cream
1 tbsp brandy
leaves from 1 bunch English spinach
1 tbsp extra virgin olive oil
2 garlic cloves, finely chopped
3 cups cooked Japanese short-grain rice
4 slices camembert cheese, to serve
2 tsp chilli and garlic oil (Pantry, page 19), optional

1. Toss the chicken with the stir-fry marinade. Heat the olive oil in a wok over high heat, add the chicken and stir-fry for about 3 minutes until well browned. Add the onion and toss for 30 seconds. Add the mushrooms, salt and pepper and toss again for 1 minute. Add the mentsuyu and cream and continue to stir-fry until the sauce thickens slightly. Flambé with the brandy and cook for another 30 seconds to ensure all the alcohol evaporates. Set aside.

2. Wash the spinach leaves well and add the wet leaves and 1 tablespoon of water to a saucepan over medium heat. Cover and cook for 3–5 minutes until wilted and very tender. Cool slightly and gently squeeze out the water with your hands. Purée in a food processor or pass the spinach through a tamis sieve (see Note) and set aside.

3. Add the oil to the wok and heat over medium-high heat until nearly smoking. Add the garlic and stir-fry for 20–30 seconds until fragrant. Add the rice and spinach and stir-fry until all the grains of rice are coated with spinach and garlic.

4. To serve, spoon the rice into bowls and top with the chicken mixture. Add 2 slices of camembert to each bowl and allow to melt slightly. Serve with a small dollop of chilli and garlic oil, if you like.

Note: *A tamis sieve, also known as a drum sieve, is a mesh screen stretched flat across the bottom of an outer ring (rather than a round-bottomed or conical sieve). Put the spinach in the sieve and scrape with a flat scraper to pass it through the mesh.*

Eating lamb in Australia is no longer just about legs and shanks. Secondary cuts of lamb are delicious and moist when properly cooked and they are well worth the effort to source and try. Ribs are perfect for this dish, but you could also try lamb belly or lamb flaps for something a little more decadent.

Lamb ribs with green chilli and herb relish

Serves: 4–6
Preparation: 25 minutes
Cooking: about 2 hours + 20 minutes resting

4 racks of lamb ribs

Green chilli and herb relish
1 whole coriander plant (see Note)
1 large handful mint leaves
6 shiso leaves
3 large green chillies, seeds removed, roughly
   chopped
2 garlic cloves
1 tbsp fish sauce
1 tsp caster sugar
2 tbsp rice wine vinegar
2 tsp yuzu juice (or substitute lemon juice)

1. Preheat the oven to 140°C. Season the lamb ribs with sea salt and place on a rack in a shallow baking dish. Pour about 2cm hot water into the dish. Roast the lamb for 1¾–2 hours until crisp and brown outside and tender and moist inside. Rest for 20 minutes and then cut into portions.

2. To make the relish, mix all the ingredients in a food processor until smooth. Serve with the lamb ribs.

Note: *Use a coriander plant (stems, leaves and root attached), not a bunch of coriander.*

This is a very simple soup that I eat with ridiculous regularity. Once the soup stock is made and the vegetables are prepared (and they will keep for quite a few days in the fridge) it's only minutes away from being ready. Fast, nourishing, healthy and rehydrating — this is my perfect breakfast and because it is so quick it leaves me with plenty of time in the mornings. I think a slice or two of kaya toast (page 102) followed by this broth gets the day off to a great start.

Breakfast broth

Serves: 3–4
Preparation: 15 minutes
Cooking: 5 minutes

1.25 litres everyday soup stock (Pantry, page 14)
1 tsp sea salt flakes
8 Chinese fish balls (see Note)
4 fresh shiitake mushrooms
½ bunch Chinese spinach (about 170g), washed
1 small bunch (about 100g) fresh enoki mushrooms
100g silken tofu, drained and cut into 1.5cm cubes
white pepper and fried shallots, to serve

1. Bring the stock and salt to a simmer in a large saucepan. Cut the fish balls in half and add to the stock.

2. Remove the stalks from the shiitake mushrooms (see Note) and cut the caps in half. Separate the spinach stalks and leaves and cut into 5cm lengths.

3. Add the shiitake caps, spinach stalks and enoki mushrooms to the pan. Simmer for 30 seconds and then add the tofu and spinach leaves. Simmer for 1–2 minutes until the mushrooms and spinach are tender.

4. Serve in bowls and top with white pepper and fried shallots.

....

Note: *Chinese fish balls are usually bought frozen — there is no need to thaw them before use. Fresh shiitake stalks pack loads of great earthy flavour. You can cut off the hard end and finely slice the rest of the stalk to add to the soup, but be sure to simmer the soup a little longer until the stalks are tender. I prefer to skewer them and grill them with just a little salt and a squeeze of lemon juice.*

This sea urchin butter recipe is from my good friend Matthew Crabbe. He serves it at his Tokyo restaurant, Two Rooms, and it is a huge hit. The butter is great with steak, fish or scallops, but here I'm serving it with lobster, just to be a bit fancy.

Poached lobster with sea urchin butter

Serves: 2–4
Preparation: 20 minutes
Cooking: 14 minutes per kg + 1 hour freezing

2 litres ichiban dashi (Pantry, page 15), other stock, salted water or shellfish nage, for poaching
1 large live lobster or crayfish, weighed, frozen for 1 hour (see Note)

Sea urchin butter
150g unsalted butter, softened
50g fresh sea urchin roe
2 tsp dijon mustard
½ bunch chives, chopped
2 tsp light soy sauce

1. To make the sea urchin butter, beat the butter with electric beaters until completely white. Add the sea urchin roe and continue to whip until no lumps remain. Add the mustard, chives and soy sauce and whip until well combined. Wrap in plastic wrap and shape into a log about 25cm long. Place in the fridge or freezer until firm.

2. Bring the poaching stock to the boil. Add the lobster to the pot over high heat and bring back to the boil. Reduce the heat so the stock is just simmering, then poach the lobster for 10 minutes for the first 500g and 1 minute for every additional 125g or part thereof. For example, a 1kg lobster would be cooked for 14 minutes.

3. Drain the lobster and cut in half lengthways.

4. Thickly slice the sea urchin butter and bring to room temperature. Top the lobster with the butter and gratinée with a blowtorch or under a very hot grill until lightly browned. Serve immediately.

Note: *To calculate cooking times you need to know the weight of your lobster before freezing. Freezing the lobster for 1 hour is the most humane way to treat it before boiling. Don't leave it in the freezer any longer than an hour or the flesh will become frozen.*

This is a great little salad that works really well with any number of dishes. Raw corn is something I love but it's very much underused. Sweet, crunchy and bursting with flavour, raw corn is a summer staple for me. Try it, and you may not go back to cooking corn for a while.

Raw corn and carrot salad

Serves: 2–4
Preparation: 20 minutes + 30 minutes chilling

½ small carrot
½ red onion
2 corn cobs

Dressing
2 tbsp Kewpie mayonnaise
1 tbsp yoghurt
1 tbsp lemon juice
2 tsp honey
1 tsp harissa
¼ tsp ground cumin
¼ tsp ground turmeric

1. To make the dressing, mix together all the ingredients, season with a pinch of black pepper and sea salt and leave in the fridge for 30 minutes for the flavours to blend.

2. Peel the carrot and cut into 5mm cubes. Finely dice the onion. Run a knife down the corn cobs to strip away the kernels. Toss all the ingredients together with the dressing and serve.

This is my 'new kitchen' version of the classic chirashi zushi. The cold smoked kingfish has a lovely caramel flavour from the brown sugar, while the two jellies add bursts of freshness and flavour.

Smoked kingfish chirashi zushi with green tea and yuzu jellies

Serves: 2
Preparation: 40 minutes
Cooking: 25 minutes + 30 minutes setting

100g snow peas, trimmed
3 cups cooked sushi rice (On Sushi, page 34)
3 tbsp white sesame seeds, toasted
1 sheet nori, toasted and crumbled
2 tsp salmon roe
chervil sprigs and shiso cress, to serve

Cold-smoked kingfish
200g kingfish fillets
2 tbsp green tea leaves (not powder)
2 tbsp brown sugar
2 tbsp uncooked rice

Shiitake mushrooms
10 dried shiitake mushrooms
125ml ichiban dashi (Pantry, page 15)
1½ tbsp caster sugar
1 tbsp sake
2 tbsp mirin
2 tbsp light soy sauce

Kinishi tamago
2 eggs
1 tsp caster sugar
1 tsp neutral-flavoured oil

Yuzu jelly
50ml yuzu juice
200ml water
1 tbsp caster sugar
1½ tsp agar agar powder
½ tsp bicarbonate of soda

Green tea jelly
250ml water
¼ tsp green tea powder
1½ tsp agar agar powder

1. For the cold smoked kingfish, remove the skin and bloodline from the fish. Line the base of a wok with a double layer of foil and add the tea leaves, brown sugar and rice. Heat over high heat until beginning to smoke. (You can quicken this by simultaneously burning the top of the mixture with a blowtorch.) When the mixture is smoking, turn off the heat and place an oiled rack in the wok about 6cm from the top of the smoke mixture. Put the fish on the rack and cover the wok tightly. Cold smoke the fish for 6 minutes (it will still be raw), then refrigerate.

2. To prepare the shiitake mushrooms, rinse and place in a heatproof bowl. Cover with boiling water and leave to soak for 30 minutes. Remove the hard stalks and thinly slice the caps. Add to a small saucepan with the dashi, sugar, sake, mirin and soy sauce and simmer for 10 minutes until all the liquid has evaporated. Set aside to cool.

3. For the kinishi tamago, break the egg yolks with chopsticks or a fork and mix gently with the whites (do not whisk or there will be too much air in the mixture). Pass through a sieve, then mix in the sugar and a pinch of salt. Heat a small frying pan over medium heat, brush with a little oil and pour in a little of the egg, tilting the pan to make a very thin omelette. When just set, flip over and heat until cooked through but not browned. Drain on paper towel. Cook the rest of the omelettes (about 3), then roll up and slice thinly.

4. To make the yuzu jelly, lightly grease a 26 x 16cm tin and line with plastic freezer wrap or cling wrap (freezer wrap gives a smoother finish). Mix the ingredients in a saucepan and bring to the boil, whisking. Reduce heat to a simmer and continue to whisk for about 5 minutes. Pour into the lined tin and refrigerate for 30 minutes until set. For the green tea jelly, use the same method and pour into a separate tin to set. When set, cut the jellies into 5mm cubes.

5. Slice the kingfish thinly and bring to room temperature. Blanch the snow peas in boiling salted water for 1–2 minutes, drain, then plunge into iced water. Drain again, pat dry with paper towel and slice thinly on an angle.

6. To serve, mix the sushi rice with the sesame seeds, nori and shiitake mushrooms. Lay kingfish over the rice and scatter with a tablespoon of each of the jellies and the salmon roe. Garnish with chervil and shiso cress.

This collection of skewers is inspired by the 'Shichifukujin', the Seven Lucky Gods of Japan. Each skewer represents a specific god and their attributes and influences. Serve them in the order printed here. You will need 6 small bamboo skewers for each of these recipes. Soak them for at least 20 minutes in cold water before use, to prevent them burning on the grill. Cook these on a preheated yakitori grill or barbecue.

Seven lucky gods

Makes: 42 skewers
Preparation: 1 hour
Cooking: about 30 minutes

Ebisu (god of fishing and good fortune)

300g sashimi-grade tuna, cut into strips 2cm thick
1 tbs liquid from pickled ginger
1 egg
1 tsp caster sugar
2 tbsp yuzu juice
300ml grapeseed oil
½ avocado, chopped
pickled ginger, to serve

1. Season the tuna. Sear the tuna for a few seconds on each side, cover and refrigerate.

2. Combine the ginger liquid, egg, sugar and yuzu juice in a small food processor. With the motor running, slowly add the oil until the mixture is thick and creamy. Add the avocado and mix again. Season to taste and refrigerate for up to 30 minutes.

3. Cut the tuna into cubes and thread onto the soaked skewers. Serve with the pickled ginger and avocado mayonnaise.

Benzaiten (goddess of music and art)

200ml grapeseed oil
½ onion, diced
2 tbsp ground turmeric
1 tsp chilli powder
1 tsp salt
6 large scallops, without roe
green chilli and herb relish, to serve (page 176)

1. Combine the oil, onion, turmeric, chilli powder and salt in a small saucepan and cook, stirring occasionally, over medium-low heat for about 5 minutes until the onion is soft. Cook for a further 35 minutes, using a deep-frying thermometer to ensure the oil temperature stays between 100°C and 122°C. Cool, then strain.

2. Thread the scallops onto skewers and sear for 30 seconds on each side. Serve with the turmeric oil and the relish.

Daidokuten (god of harvest and kitchen)

6 large fresh shiitake mushrooms with thick stems, ends trimmed
6 asparagus tips
vegetable oil
1 thin slice lemon, cut into 6 pieces

1. Separate the mushroom caps and stalks. Thread a stalk and a cap onto each skewer. Brush the mushrooms and the asparagus tips with oil, season well with salt and grill for about 3 minutes, turning often, until browned and the asparagus is tender-crisp. Serve with a piece of lemon.

Hotei (god of contentment and happiness)

2 tsp green tea powder
3 tsp sea salt
2 tsp Sichuan peppercorns
250g boneless pork belly, cut
    into 18 slices (1 x 3cm)

1. Grind the green tea and salt to a fine
   powder with a mortar and pestle. Toast the
   peppercorns in a dry frying pan over medium
   heat for 2 minutes. Cool slightly and grind to a
   fine powder.

2. Thread the pork lengthways onto skewers.
   Grill for 8 minutes, turning occasionally. Serve
   sprinkled with the green tea salt and ground
   Sichuan pepper.

Jurojin (god of longevity)

200g venison fillet, thickly sliced
60ml sake
1 tsp ground white pepper
6 shiso leaves
2 umeboshi (salted plums), finely chopped

1. Place the venison in a non-reactive bowl with
   the sake and pepper and marinate for
   30 minutes. Drain, and season with salt.

2. Thread the venison onto skewers and grill
   for 3 minutes for medium–rare, turning once.
   Serve on shiso leaves with the umeboshi.

Bishamonten (god of war and warriors)

400g wagyu beef short ribs, bones and excess
    fat discarded
2 tsp fresh grated wasabi
1 small handful pea shoots

1. Cut the beef into 2cm cubes, thread onto skewers
   and season well. Grill for 3 minutes each side
   for medium–rare.

2. Dot with a little wasabi and sprinkle
   with pea shoots to serve.

Fukurokuju (god of wisdom)

125ml soy sauce
2 tbsp sake
60ml mirin
55g sugar
1 tsp dashi powder
1 tbsp molasses
2 leeks, inner white leaves only
3 chicken thigh fillets, cut into 3cm pieces
shichimi togarishi, to serve

1. Combine the soy sauce, sake, mirin, sugar, dashi
   and molasses in a small saucepan. Stir over low
   heat until the sugar has dissolved. Leave to cool.

2. Cut the leek into 3cm lengths. Thread 1 piece of
   leek, 2 pieces of chicken and another piece of leek
   onto each skewer. Brush with the sauce and grill
   for 5 minutes on each side or until well browned
   and cooked through, brushing often with the
   sauce. Serve with the shichimi togarishi.

Lamb fried with cumin is a classic northern Chinese dish. I have used the traditional flavours in a kind of warm salad teamed with some wonderful fresh herbs and a peanut relish for texture.

Chilli cumin lamb with peanuts and herbs

Serves: 2
Preparation: 20 minutes
Cooking: 8 minutes

vegetable oil, to deep-fry
300g lamb topside, cut into 2cm cubes
1 tbsp cornflour
2 tbsp neutral-flavoured oil
40g raw peanuts, peeled
½ brown onion, finely diced
2 garlic cloves, chopped
1 tbsp dark soy sauce
¼ tsp caster sugar, plus an extra pinch
5 dried chillies, stalks and seeds removed
1 tbsp cumin seeds
1 tsp chilli powder
¼ tsp sea salt flakes
2 large handfuls mint leaves
1 large handful coriander leaves
lemon wedges and cooked rice, to serve

1. Half-fill a wok with vegetable oil and heat to 180°C. Toss the lamb in the cornflour and deep-fry for 3–5 minutes until well browned. Lift out with a slotted spoon and drain on paper towel. Drain the vegetable oil from the wok.

2. Heat half the neutral oil in the wok and stir-fry the peanuts until golden brown. Remove with a slotted spoon, drain and roughly chop. Add the onion and garlic to the wok and stir-fry for 1–2 minutes until softened and starting to colour. Add the soy sauce and sugar and stir-fry for 30 seconds. Return the peanuts to the wok with the chillies and toss for about 30 seconds. Remove the mixture from the wok and set aside.

3. Heat the remaining oil in the wok and add the cumin and chilli powder. Stir-fry for 30 seconds until fragrant. Add the lamb, the salt and a pinch of sugar. Toss for about 30 seconds and then add half the mint. When the mint has wilted, remove the lamb mixture from the wok.

4. Arrange a bed of coriander and mint leaves on a serving plate and top with the lamb mixture. Spoon the peanut and onion mixture on top of the lamb. Serve with wedges of lemon. Just before eating, squeeze on the lemon juice and toss as you would a salad. Eat with rice.

A good plate of fish and chips should never be underestimated. Here, the combination of the sweet-but-tart pickled chilli and the creamy mandarin curd works much like a tartare sauce.

Tempura fish and chips with pickled chilli mandarin curd

Serves: 4
Preparation: 30 minutes
Cooking: 30 minutes

5 large sebago potatoes (or other floury potatoes), peeled
vegetable oil, to deep-fry
400g flathead fillets (or other firm white fish)
1 quantity tempura batter (On tempura, page 41)

Pickled chilli mandarin curd
3 mandarins
2 lemons
1 egg plus 5 egg yolks
200g unsalted butter, chopped
¼ tsp sea salt flakes
2 tbsp pickled chillies (Pantry, page 23)

1. To make the curd, finely grate the zest of the mandarins and lemons and squeeze the juice to yield about 200ml in total. Combine the egg and yolks with the zest and juice in a small saucepan. Add half the butter and whisk over low heat until melted, then add the remaining butter. Continue to whisk over low heat for about 6–8 minutes until just thickened. Do not allow the mixture to get too hot or the eggs will curdle. Remove from the heat and whisk until cool. Season with salt. Set a few pickled chillies aside to scatter on the top and stir the rest into the curd.

2. Cut the potatoes into thick chips. Half-fill a large saucepan with oil and heat to 140°C. Deep-fry the potatoes in 2 batches until just starting to brown at the edges. Lift out with a slotted spoon and drain on paper towel. Spread out into a single layer and set aside to dry and cool.

3. Increase the heat until the deep-frying oil reaches 190°C. Deep-fry the chips again in 2 batches until golden brown and crispy. Season well with salt and keep warm in a low oven.

4. Reduce the oil temperature to 160°C. Dip the fish in tempura batter and fry in 2 batches for 4–5 minutes until cooked through. Drain on paper towel. Serve with the chips and curd.

Ginger and teriyaki are a classic combination in Japanese cuisine. Teriyaki is a great glaze for most meat and seafood, but here I have used the meaty, gamey flavour of quail, which matches really well with the pungency of the raw ginger. You can serve this as it is as part of a shared meal, or team it with some cooked rice and greens for a one-plate main course.

Teriyaki quail with raw ginger

Serves: 2
Preparation: 10 minutes
Cooking: 6 minutes

1 tbsp neutral-flavoured oil
2 whole quail, deboned (see Note) and butterflied
100ml teriyaki glaze (Pantry, page 27)
sea salt flakes, to taste
1 tsp finely grated ginger

1. Heat a large frying pan over medium heat and add the oil. When the oil is hot but not smoking, add the quail. Sear quickly on both sides. Reduce the heat to low and cook, turning every 30 seconds, for about 4 minutes.

2. Add the glaze to the pan and continue to turn the birds in the glaze for about 2 minutes until the glaze thickens and has coated the birds. Transfer the quail to a plate, pour any pan juices and caramelised glaze over the birds and leave to rest for 2 minutes.

3. Season the quail with a little sea salt and serve with the ginger.

Note: *Remove all bones from the quail except the drumette bone in the wing and the lowest leg bone. Open out the quail, breast-side-up, and press the breast gently to flatten.*

The crispy grilled tofu in this dish adds a wonderful texture when contrasted with the gooey melted cheese. The sweet dengaku miso sauce completes the experience. The sauce is also wonderful with eggplant.

Tofu and camembert skewers with dengaku miso

Makes: 4 skewers
Preparation: 20 minutes
Cooking: 10 minutes

8 deep-fried tofu puffs
100g camembert cheese, cut into large cubes
2 spring onions, finely sliced
black sesame seeds, to serve

Dengaku miso
3 tbsp hatcho miso
1 tbsp sugar
2 tbsp mirin
3 tbsp ichiban dashi (Pantry, page 15)
1 tbsp sake

1. Soak 4 bamboo skewers in water for at least 20 minutes to prevent them scorching during grilling. To make the dengaku miso, combine all the ingredients in a saucepan and stir over low heat until thickened. Set aside.

2. Split the tofu puffs almost in half but not all the way through. Open up like Pac-Man and hollow out about half of each side with your fingers. Put a large cube of camembert inside, followed by a pinch of sliced spring onion. Secure with a skewer (2 tofu puffs per skewer).

3. Grill the skewers on a yakitori grill or under a preheated grill for about 2–3 minutes until the tofu puff is just crisp on the outside and the camembert melting into the spring onion. Do not grill for too long or the camembert will melt away and you will be left with a hollow puff.

4. Spread the skewers with a thick layer of the dengaku miso and scatter with sesame seeds.

Fried egg and tomato is a hugely popular mainland Chinese dish that is rarely seen outside of China. Very simply fried with salt and a little pepper, it's hard to improve on something so delicious. For this rice bowl I've taken the elegant simplicity of this dish and teamed it with beautiful heirloom tomatoes, whose unique flavours and colours really benefit from this simple treatment.

Egg and heirloom tomato rice bowl

Serves: 2
Preparation: 5 minutes + 10 minutes standing
Cooking: 1 minute

2 large ripe heirloom tomatoes, cut into thick wedges
½ tsp sea salt flakes
1 pinch white pepper
4 eggs, lightly beaten
2 tbsp neutral-flavoured oil
3 spring onions, green part only, finely sliced
3 cups cooked Japanese short-grain rice

1. Scatter the tomatoes with the salt and pepper and leave for 10 minutes. Mix together the egg and any juice from the tomatoes. Heat the oil in a wok over medium-high heat until smoking and then add the eggs. Leave to cook for 20 seconds, then add the tomatoes on top of the eggs. When the egg is half-cooked, toss the wok to combine the egg and tomatoes.

2. Continue to stir-fry until the egg is nearly set but still a little runny and the tomatoes have just softened. Mix in the spring onions and then immediately serve over bowls of cooked rice.

This dish shows an interesting Japanese technique of seasoning fried food by dipping it into a flavoured liquid after cooking. The food loses some of its crisp finish but takes up the flavour of the seasoning liquid.

Black vinegar chicken nanban

Serves: 2
Preparation: 30 minutes
Cooking: 10 minutes + 15 minutes standing

neutral-flavoured oil, to deep-fry
2 chicken thigh fillets
3 tbsp cornflour
2 eggs, lightly beaten

Black vinegar nanbanzuke
100ml dark soy sauce
120ml Chinkiang black vinegar
3 tbsp caster sugar
½ tsp salt
1 tsp chilli and garlic oil (Pantry, page 19)

Tartare sauce
½ cup Kewpie mayonnaise
1 hard-boiled egg yolk, pressed through a sieve
1 tbsp finely chopped capers
1 tbsp finely diced brown onion
1 tbsp finely diced dill pickle
1 tsp finely chopped flat-leaf parsley
1 tsp finely chopped chives
1 tsp lemon juice

1. To make the black vinegar nanbanzuke seasoning liquid, combine all the ingredients in a saucepan and stir over low heat to dissolve the sugar. Transfer to a deep tray or bowl.

2. To make the tartare sauce, mix together all the ingredients in a bowl.

3. Half-fill a large saucepan with oil and heat to 180°C. Dip the chicken into the cornflour and shake off any excess. Dip into the egg and then back into the cornflour.

4. Deep-fry the chicken for about 10 minutes until golden. Lift out of the oil, letting the oil drain off. Put the chicken into the seasoning liquid and leave for 15 minutes, turning once.

5. Slice the chicken and serve with the tartare sauce.

Shiitake mushrooms have an almost magical quality. The intense umami flavour of dried shiitake is not often found in their fresh counterparts but, when lightly grilled, they have a strong savoury perfume that is truly amazing. I have seasoned these mushroom skewers with a beautifully fragrant powder made from dried preserved lemon.

Shiitake mushroom skewers with preserved lemon powder

Makes: 6 skewers
Preparation: 15 minutes
Cooking: 4 hours + 5 minutes

1 preserved lemon
8 fresh shiitake mushrooms, caps and stalks
   (choose mushrooms with thick, tender stalks)
a little neutral-flavoured oil, for brushing

1. Preheat the oven to 60°C. Remove the pulp and pith from the preserved lemon and julienne the zest. Spread on a tray lined with baking paper and bake for at least 4 hours or until very dry and brittle. Grind to a powder with a mortar and pestle. Meanwhile, soak 6 bamboo skewers in water for at least 20 minutes so they don't scorch during cooking.

2. Separate the stalks from the mushroom caps and trim away any woody ends from the stalks. Thread the mushroom caps and stalks on the skewers — 2 caps per skewer or 4 stalks per skewer. Brush with a little oil, season with a little salt and grill (on a yakitori grill or under a preheated grill) for about 2–3 minutes each side until softened and slightly charred.

3. Sprinkle with preserved lemon powder to serve.

Bacon and cherry tomato skewers are a modern dish that can be found in many yakitori restaurants around Tokyo. They have always reminded me of the 1960s cocktail party classic, devils on horseback, so this dish features sweet elements of dried fruit with the warm sultana vinaigrette.

Bacon and cherry tomato skewers with warm sultana vinaigrette

Makes: 6 skewers
Preparation: 15 minutes
Cooking: 20 minutes

3 rashers middle bacon
12 small cherry tomatoes (or grape tomatoes)

Warm sultana vinaigrette
2 tbsp tentsuyu (Pantry, page 26)
50g sultanas, roughly chopped
2 tsp rice wine vinegar
1 tsp chopped flat-leaf parsley

1. To make the vinaigrette, warm the tentsuyu in a small saucepan and add the sultanas. Remove from the heat and leave to cool slightly. Stir in the vinegar and parsley while the sultanas are still warm. Meanwhile, soak 6 bamboo skewers in water for at least 20 minutes so they don't scorch during cooking.

2. Trim any rind from the bacon and cut the streaky section into two 10cm lengths. Cut the eye of the bacon in half lengthways — this should leave you with twelve 10cm lengths of bacon.

3. Wrap each tomato in a piece of bacon and thread 2 onto each skewer, using the skewers to hold the bacon in place. Grill until the bacon is cooked and the tomatoes slightly softened — if you don't have a yakitori grill you can cook these under a grill or bake in a 200°C oven for about 20 minutes.

4. Serve the skewers with the warm vinaigrette.

Fresh sugar cane is something that's easy to fall in love with. The super sweet juice can sometimes be overpowering, but here I've used it to make a rich ice cream that really brings out its fresh and unique characteristics. Sugar cane is quite easily found in Australia (we're a major producer of sugar) and is relatively simple to extract. Remove the hard outer layer (or use canned sugar cane with this already done) and then use a domestic juicer or food processor to extract the sweet liquid.

Sugar cane ice cream

Makes: about 500ml
Preparation: 15 minutes
Cooking: about 10 minutes + overnight freezing

3 egg yolks
50g caster sugar
100ml milk
150ml sugar cane juice (see Note)
100ml pouring cream

1. Whisk the egg yolks and sugar in a metal bowl until slightly pale. Scald the milk by bringing it just to boiling point and immediately pour it onto the egg yolks and caster sugar. Whisk in a double boiler or a bowl placed over a pan of barely simmering water for about 10 minutes until pale, thickened and doubled in volume. Don't let the mixture get too hot or it will curdle.

2. Whisk the sugar cane juice and cream into the mixture. Churn in an ice-cream maker according to the manufacturer's directions, then transfer to an airtight container and freeze overnight.

3. Serve the ice cream by itself, with fresh fruit, or as an accompaniment to sataa andagi (page 133).

Note: *Sugar cane juice is available in most Asian shops (avoid the sugar cane 'drink'). If you can't find it, extract the juice from canned sugar cane by finely chopping three 15cm lengths of sugar cane in a food processor and then squeezing the chopped pulp through a layer of muslin to produce juice. Alternatively, use a commercial juicer.*

Farmers Union iced coffee is a South Australian icon, and with good reason. This dish takes the defining drink of my teenage years and converts it into an elegant dessert.

Farmers Union iced coffee pudding with tea-smoked chocolate and five-spice tenkasu

Makes: 4
Preparation: 30 minutes
Cooking: about 15 minutes + 2 hours setting

50g soft brown sugar
50g lapsang souchong tea leaves
300g couverture chocolate (75% cacao)
¼ tsp Chinese five-spice powder
2 tsp icing sugar
1 cup tenkasu (On tempura, page 41)

Iced coffee pudding
3 leaves titanium-strength gelatine
600ml Farmers Union iced coffee
150ml pouring cream
1 tbsp caster sugar

1. To make the pudding, soak the gelatine in a bowl of cold water for about 3 minutes to soften. Heat the iced coffee, cream and sugar over low heat, stirring, until just warm and the sugar has dissolved. Squeeze out the water from the gelatine and add to the iced coffee mixture. Stir until completely dissolved. Pour into four 200ml glasses and refrigerate for about 2 hours to set.

2. Line the base of a wok with foil and sprinkle with the sugar and tea. Place a rack in the wok with a tray over the top. Break the chocolate into chunks and put 200g in a heatproof bowl. Heat the wok until the tea leaves and sugar are smoking and then turn off the heat and place the bowl on the rack. Cover the wok and leave for 5–10 minutes until the chocolate has melted. Take the temperature of the chocolate. If it is not 45°C then heat it briefly over a double boiler.

3. Add the remaining chocolate a few pieces at a time until they melt and the temperature of the chocolate drops to around 27°C. Pour the chocolate onto a marble slab to set and then scrape with a pastry scraper into curls and shards.

4. Sift together the five-spice powder and icing sugar and toss through the tenkasu to coat.

5. To serve, top the puddings with tenkasu and shards of smoked chocolate.

In this dessert the delicate perfume of a simple lemongrass and rambutan sorbet is offset by the slight saltiness of a bavarois made with evaporated milk.

Evaporated milk bavarois with lemongrass and rambutan sorbet

Serves: 8
Preparation: 40 minutes
Cooking: 5 minutes + overnight freezing
  + 3 hours setting

1 starfruit (carambola), sliced
1 tbsp caster sugar

Bavarois
2 titanium-strength gelatine leaves
3 egg yolks
100g caster sugar
300ml evaporated milk
250ml thickened cream

Lemongrass and rambutan sorbet
2 stalks lemongrass, white part only, lightly crushed
80g caster sugar (see Note)
40g glucose
350g puréed rambutans (fresh or canned)

1. To make the sorbet, put the lemongrass in a small saucepan with the sugar, glucose and 150ml water. Stir over low heat without boiling until the sugar has dissolved. Bring to the boil and then set aside for 30 minutes to cool and infuse. Stir in the rambutan purée and a pinch of salt and churn in an ice-cream machine according to the manufacturer's instructions. Transfer to an airtight container and freeze overnight.

2. To make the bavarois, soak the gelatine in a bowl of cold water for about 3 minutes to soften. Whisk the egg yolks and sugar together until thick and pale. Scald the evaporated milk by bringing just to boiling point and then strain onto the egg yolks, whisking continuously. Squeeze the water from the gelatine and whisk into the milk mixture until completely dissolved. Leave for about 10 minutes, stirring occasionally to release the heat, until just lukewarm. Beat the cream to soft peaks and gently whisk into the milk mixture. Pour into 8 lightly oiled 125ml dariole or jelly moulds and set in the fridge for about 3 hours.

3. Sprinkle the starfruit with sugar. Cook in a dry non-stick frying pan over medium-high heat for about 2 minutes each side until caramelised.

4. Turn out the bavarois onto serving plates. Serve with the sorbet and caramelised starfruit.

Note: *Reduce the sugar in the sorbet to 50g if you are using canned rambutans in syrup.*

Red bean desserts originated in China but are now very common in many Asian cultures. I think they're delicious, but the sticky texture of red bean paste is not to everyone's taste. I've often thought of the texture as akin to very soft fudge and so, after tasting some amazing whisky fudge at my sister's wedding in Scotland, I came up with this idea.

Red bean fudge

Makes: 30
Preparation: 20 minutes + overnight soaking
Cooking: 1 hour 40 minutes

Red bean purée
60g dried red beans
½ tsp finely grated orange zest
½ tsp vanilla paste (or seeds scraped from
    ½ vanilla bean)

Basic fudge
80g unsalted butter
450g caster sugar
150ml milk
300ml pouring cream

1. Soak the red beans overnight in cold water. Drain and cover with ample cold water in a large saucepan. Bring to the boil and then reduce the heat and simmer for 40 minutes until the beans are tender. Drain the beans and purée in a food processor. Return the purée to the warm dry pan and cook over low heat, stirring continuously, for a few minutes until much of the water has evaporated. Beat in the orange zest, vanilla paste and a pinch of salt and set aside to cool.

2. Lightly grease a 10 x 20cm loaf tin and line with baking paper.

3. To make the fudge, stir the butter and 60ml water in a large deep saucepan until the butter has melted. Add the sugar, milk and cream and stir without boiling until the sugar has dissolved. Brush down the side of the pan with cold water to dissolve any sugar crystals.

4. Bring to the boil over high heat. Reduce the heat to medium and cook for about 40 minutes or until the mixture reaches 110°C on a sugar thermometer (see Note).

5. Whisk the red bean mixture into the fudge, return to the boil and continue cooking until the mixture reaches 114°C on the thermometer (until a little of the mixture, dropped into cold water, can be shaped into a soft ball). Remove from the heat and beat with a wooden spoon until pale and very thick. Pour into the tray and cool to room temperature. Cut into squares to serve. Great with a green tea latte.

Note: *Keep your eye on the mixture as it can boil over. You will need to adjust the heat to keep it cooking at a level where it will not overflow — depending on your particular saucepan, the cooking time may differ.*

The tropical flavours of mango, coconut and macadamia come together in this dish. The ice cream smells and tastes like a deliciously edible version of sunscreen. For me, it's just like a day at the beach.

Mango sun pies with sunscreen ice cream

Serves: 6
Preparation: 40 minutes
Cooking: 35 minutes + churning + overnight freezing

Sunscreen ice cream
100ml macadamia oil
150ml milk
100ml coconut cream
1 tsp coconut essence
¼ tsp vanilla paste (or seeds scraped from
    ½ vanilla bean)
3 egg yolks
100g caster sugar
300ml pouring cream

Mango sun pies
300g granita biscuits
40g almond meal
1½ tbsp caster sugar
125g butter, melted
500ml fresh mango purée (see Note)
5 eggs, lightly beaten
395g condensed milk
160ml pouring cream
juice and finely grated zest of ½ lemon

1. To make the ice cream, combine the oil, milk, coconut cream, coconut essence and vanilla paste in a small saucepan. Bring just to the boil then remove from the heat. Whisk the egg yolks and sugar in a large bowl until pale and creamy. Gradually pour in the hot milk mixture, whisking continuously. Wash and dry the pan, then strain the mixture back into the pan. Stir continuously over low heat without boiling for 10 minutes or until the mixture coats the back of spoon. Pour into a plastic container and refrigerate for about 1½ hours until chilled.

2. Beat the cream to soft peaks and fold through the chilled mixture. Churn in an ice-cream machine according to manufacturer's instructions, then transfer to an airtight container and freeze overnight.

3. To make the mango sun pies, preheat the oven to 160°C. Line the bases of six 10cm springform tins with baking paper (see Note). Process the biscuits to coarse crumbs. Add the almond meal, sugar and butter and process until combined. Press the mixture firmly into the base and up the sides of the tins. Refrigerate for 20 minutes, until firm.

4. Whisk the mango purée with the eggs, condensed milk, cream, lemon juice and zest until smooth. Pour into the tins and bake for 25 minutes until just set and still slightly wobbly in the centre. Cool and serve with sunscreen ice cream.

Note: *You will need about 4 ripe mangoes, flesh puréed and passed through a sieve. You can make one 23cm tart if you prefer; it will take 40–45 minutes to cook.*

I made this dessert for a function I was hosting in the Australia Pavilion at the 2010 Shanghai World Expo. It was the clear hit of the day and I was inundated with requests for the recipe. The tofu adds a slight acidity and lightness to the cream cheese to give a dessert that is not too sweet or heavy but still luxurious. And the buttery texture of the brioche croutons is to die for.

Tofu cheese mousse

Serves: 4
Preparation: 30 minutes
Cooking: 10 minutes + 2 hours setting

100ml orange blossom water
3 tbsp sultanas
2 thick slices brioche
1 tbs unsalted butter
leatherwood honey and chervil sprigs, to serve

Mousse
300ml pouring cream
100g cream cheese
200g silken tofu
2 sheets titanium-strength gelatine
4 tbsp icing sugar

1. To make the mousse, beat the cream to soft peaks and set aside to come to room temperature. Meanwhile, mash the cream cheese and tofu in a metal bowl and place over a saucepan of simmering water. Stir until quite warm and then whisk until smooth. Meanwhile, soak the gelatine in a bowl of cold water for about 3 minutes to soften, then squeeze out the excess water and add to the tofu mixture with the icing sugar. Whisk until the gelatine has dissolved.

2. Remove the bowl from the heat and let the mixture cool to room temperature for 10 minutes. It will thicken slightly. Gently fold in the whipped cream and then pour into four 125ml dariole moulds. Refrigerate for about 2 hours until set.

3. Put the orange blossom water in a saucepan with 50ml water and heat to just below boiling point. Add the sultanas and then set aside for at least 10 minutes until plump and cool. Remove the sultanas from any remaining liquid and chill, covered, in the fridge.

4. Remove the crusts from the brioche and cut into large batons about 2 x 5cm. Heat the butter in a frying pan and fry the brioche batons until coloured on all sides and ends.

5. Unmould the mousse by dipping each mould into hot water, then turning out onto serving plates. Drizzle with a little honey, scatter with the sultanas and chervil and serve with the croutons.

A fool is a wonderfully simple English dessert of fruit purée folded through whipped cream. The green tea meringue in this version adds another texture and the freshness of the mandarin segments lightens the whole arrangement.

Green tea meringue and mandarin fool

Serves: 4–6
Preparation: 30 minutes
Cooking: 1 hour + chilling

2 mandarins, segmented, deseeded and
   roughly chopped
200ml pouring cream

Green tea meringue
2 egg whites, at room temperature
110g caster sugar
1½ tsp green tea powder
½ tsp white vinegar

Mandarin custard
70ml mandarin juice
2 tsp cornflour
2 tsp finely grated mandarin zest
3 tbsp rice malt syrup
3 egg yolks
250ml pouring cream
1 tsp mandarin liqueur or Grand Marnier

1. To make the green tea meringues, preheat the oven to 150°C. Grease a baking tray and line with baking paper. Using electric beaters, beat the egg whites to soft peaks (see Note). Gradually add the combined sugar and green tea, beating well after each addition, until firm and glossy. Fold in the vinegar and transfer the mixture to a piping bag fitted with a **small round** nozzle.

2. Pipe small meringues of around 5cm diameter. Put the tray into the oven and immediately reduce the heat to 100°C. Bake for 1 hour and then turn off the oven. Allow the meringues to cool and dry in the oven. When cool, transfer to a plastic bag and beat with a rolling pin to crush. Store in an airtight container.

3. To make the mandarin custard, mix the mandarin juice and cornflour to a slurry and put in a small saucepan with the remaining ingredients. Whisk constantly over low heat for 5 minutes until thickened. Transfer to a small bowl, cover the surface with cling wrap and chill in the fridge for about 2 hours.

4. Mix the chopped mandarin segments through the custard. Whip the cream to soft peaks and then gently fold through the custard and mandarin segments to create a ripple. Serve in small glasses or bowls, topped with the crumbled meringue.

Note: *When beating egg whites, make sure the bowl is clean and free of any grease, water or detergent residue. Wiping out the bowl with paper towel moistened with vinegar can help. Keep leftover meringues in an airtight container for up to 1 week.*

Sweetened green tea and whisky is a wonderfully refreshing combination commonly found in bars and karaoke parlours all around China. Here those flavours are married with a fresh melon salad for a relatively simple summer dessert.

Melon salad with green tea and whisky granita

Serves: 6–8
Preparation: 30 minutes + overnight refrigeration
Cooking: 3–5 minutes

2 tbsp caster sugar
30g glucose
2 tbsp shredded mint leaves
½ tsp ginger juice (juice squeezed from grated fresh ginger)
2 cups each of honeydew melon balls, rockmelon balls and watermelon balls

Honey and orange yoghurt
500ml Greek-style yoghurt
2 tbsp honey
1 tbsp orange zest

Green tea and whisky granita
500ml bottle sweetened green tea
50ml whisky
80g caster sugar

1. To make the honey and orange yoghurt, line a sieve with a large piece of muslin. Pour in the yoghurt. Gather the ends together and tie in a knot. Suspend the parcel from a chopstick or wooden spoon over a large bowl and leave to drain overnight in the fridge. Mix the thickened yoghurt with the honey and orange zest.

2. Meanwhile, to make the granita, combine the ingredients in a saucepan over medium heat. Stir until the sugar has dissolved, then bring to the boil and cook for 3 minutes. Transfer to a shallow tin and freeze for about 2 hours until solid, then scrape with a fork into granita crystals.

3. Stir the caster sugar, glucose, 150ml water and a pinch of salt in a saucepan over medium heat until the sugar has dissolved. Stir in the mint leaves and ginger juice and refrigerate for 1 hour until chilled. Just before serving, toss with the melon balls.

4. To serve, place a small amount of the yoghurt in the centre of each serving plate and surround with a ring of granita. Pile the melon balls on top of the yoghurt and serve immediately.

Black vinegar is something of an acquired taste, but in my experience once that taste is acquired it's hard to shake. The slightly savoury notes of the black vinegar work well with the ginger, and the simple icing is absolutely delicious.

Black vinegar cake with sour cream icing

Serves: 8–10
Preparation: 25 minutes
Cooking: 50 minutes

160g unsalted butter, cubed
400g plain flour
200g caster sugar
150g dried apricots, roughly chopped
50g glacé ginger (uncrystallised), roughly chopped
60ml Chinkiang black vinegar
300ml full-fat milk
1 tsp bicarbonate of soda

Sour cream icing
1 tsp lemon juice
50g unsalted butter, softened
150g sour cream
100g icing sugar

1. Preheat the oven to 180°C. Lightly grease a 20cm springform cake tin and line the base with baking paper.

2. Rub the butter into the flour with your fingertips until the mixture resembles coarse breadcrumbs. Add the sugar, apricots and ginger and stir to combine. Make a well in the centre.

3. Put the vinegar and milk in a saucepan and heat gently until curdled, then add the bicarbonate of soda. As it foams, immediately pour into the flour mixture and stir to combine. This all needs to happen quickly so that the reaction between the vinegar and bicarbonate does not subside.

4. Pour into the cake tin. Bake for 20 minutes, then reduce the heat to 160°C and cook for a further 30 minutes. Cool in the tin for 10 minutes, then release the side and slide onto a wire rack to cool completely.

5. To make the icing, beat all the ingredients until smooth. Spread the icing over the cooled cake, slice and serve.

Glossary

dried soy beans

benishouga
(red pickled ginger)

hatcho miso

kochujan
(Korean chilli bean paste)

lap cheong
(Chinese sausage)

pickled ginger

ice sugar

yellow rock sugar

tamarind pulp

dried red beans

belacan
(dried shrimp paste)

palm sugar

white miso

aonori

dang gui
(Chinese angelica;
Angelica sinensis)

lovage root
(chuan xiong;
Ligusticum chuanxiong)

Solomon's seal
(yu shu; *Polygonatum yuzhu*)

powdered green tea

shu di
(*Rehmannia glutinosa*)

goji berries
(ju zi; *Lycium barbarum*)

ikan bilis

tang shen
(*Codonopsis pilosula*)

licorice root
(gan cao; *Glycyrrhiza uralensis*)

dried shiitake mushrooms

dried shrimp

shichimi
(Japanese seven-spice pepper)

cassia bark

katsuoboshi
(dried bonito flakes)

The identification of Asian ingredients does not need to be intimidating. I had been cooking for many years before I even bothered to learn the proper names of many ingredients I habitually used. Within my family ingredients were often named in a strange culinary patois with reference to the brand used, the colour or even the shape of the bottle. Often my grandmother would ask for 'black sauce', 'salty vegetable' or even simply 'Maggi' and we would all know what she wanted us to fetch. These ingredients were such a standard part of our home kitchen that a change in branding or redesign of bottle could cause a lengthy pause when shopping. All these ingredients are cheap and readily available, and a brave spirit of adventure in any Asian grocery store will likely introduce you to a vast new world of ingredients and delicious opportunities.

Tianjin preserved vegetable

mirin

Otafuku sauce

awamori

Chinkiang black vinegar

sake (nihonshu)

Sriracha chilli sauce

Shaoxing wine

Kewpie mayonnaise

Cheong Chan
cooking caramel

yuzu juice

Index

An Ebury Press book
Published by Random House Australia Pty Ltd
Level 3, 100 Pacific Highway, North Sydney NSW 2060
www.randomhouse.com.au

First published by Ebury Press in 2011

Addresses for companies within the Random House Group
can be found at www.randomhouse.com.au/offices

National Library of Australia
Cataloguing-in-Publication Entry

Liaw, Adam
Two Asian kitchens.

ISBN 978 1 86471 135 6 (hbk).

Cooking, Asian

641.595

Art direction and design by Mary Callahan Design
Photography by Steve Brown Photography
Styling by Lisa La Barbera
Project editing by Jane Price
Project food editing by Tracy Rutherford
Recipe testing by Wendy Broadhurst, Wendy Quisumbing,
    Susie Wilkins and Amanda Rogers
Recipe preparation by Wendy Quisumbing and Amanda Rogers
Index by Jon Jeremy
Props kindly supplied by Izzi and Popo, Janetta Kerr Grant,
    Kris Coad, Maria Altman and Sara La Barbera
Printed and bound by C&C Offset Printing Co. Pty Ltd.

Special thanks to Janelle Bloom, Meredith Fraser from
Scanpan, Cuisinart and Global Knives, Jai Di Marco and
Andrew Myers from Coles Supermarkets and to Anthony
Stambolis and Greg Chesler from Hospitality Depot for
their kind assistance.

www.adamliaw.com

10 9 8 7 6 5 4 3 2 1